# BACK
## TO
# LIFE

WITHDRAWN FROM STOCK

*David Rogers and Dr Grahame Brown*

3 5 7 9 10 8 6 4

Vermilion, an imprint of Ebury Publishing,
20 Vauxhall Bridge Road,
London SW1V 2SA

Vermilion is part of the Penguin Random House group of companies
whose addresses can be found at global.penguinrandomhouse.com

Penguin
Random House
UK

First published in the United Kingdom by Vermilion in 2016
www.penguin.co.uk

A CIP catalogue record for this book is available from the British Library

ISBN 9781785040740

Printed and bound in Great Britain by Clays Ltd, St Ives PLC

Penguin Random House is committed to a sustainable future for our business,
our readers and our planet. This book is made from Forest Stewardship
Council® certified paper.

# Contents

**David Rogers** is a chartered physiotherapist with over 20 years' experience of helping people with musculoskeletal pain to recover function and regain their quality of life. After completing a degree in Sports Studies, in 1994 he qualified as a chartered physiotherapist from the University of Birmingham and in 2010 gained his Masters degree in Pain Science and Management from Keele University. He has worked in many different healthcare environments, including the NHS, the occupational health industry and sports medicine, and is currently playing an active role in large research trials relating to back pain. He is based at the Royal Orthopaedic Hospital in Birmingham, where he has established a combined physical and psychological treatment service for people with persistent backpain within an interdisciplinary team. His work is focused on applying a biopsychosocial approach to recovery, using cognitive behavioural principles aimed at maximising recovery. As well as his clinical work, David is a lecturer to health care professionals, occupational health providers and physiotherapy students.


**Grahame Brown** is a physician who qualified from the University of Bristol in 1979. After junior doctor hospital jobs in the NHS, he served five years as a medical officer in the Royal Air Force. On leaving the armed forces, he worked as a GP in Norwich for five years and then as a GP in Birmingham for six years. Throughout his time in general practice he developed a special interest in, and acquired postgraduate qualifications in musculoskeletal, sport & exercise medicine, occupational medicine, psychological and behavioural medicine. In 1996 he left general practice to develop a musculoskeletal, sport & exercise medicine service at the Royal Orthopaedic Hospital NHS Trust in Birmingham, where he continues to work as a specialist physician within a large multidisciplinary team. He has tutored many one-day courses throughout the UK and

Ireland, for professionals from all disciplines, on psychological approaches to accelerate healing and treating pain utilising the principles taught by the Human Givens College. He has contributed to textbooks on musculoskeletal medicine and occupational medicine and published a book in 2009: *Liberate Yourself from Pain: A Practical Guide for Sufferers.*

# Foreword

Low back pain is one of the biggest threats to a good quality of life. It causes a range of dysfunction and disability and is poorly understood by many, including those within the medical profession. Being pain-free is seen as the goal but this can be elusive, with modern medicine seeming unable to offer a solution for most patients. Spinal surgery is, in fact, very rarely indicated for non-specific low back pain and, when undertaken, is often disappointing, with most patients continuing to experience some degree of pain and usually still requiring painkillers.

As with many things, understanding a problem makes it easier to tackle. The spine is a complex structure in itself, and when addressing back pain it is also essential to understand the complexity of pain and its interactions. There is indisputable evidence that addressing the physical and psychological aspects of pain together is far more effective than treating one or the other in isolation.

Grahame Brown and David Rogers have many years' experience in managing patients with spinal pain, both individually and as part of an interdisciplinary team. They have honed techniques that help patients to identify and modify the beliefs and fears that have added to functional restrictions, whilst at the same time helping them to improve physically. The results obtained have been impressive and are published in medical literature. Their combined 'biopsychosocial' approach addresses the range of issues that contribute to the pain experience, and gives patients skills that will continue to be useful should symptoms recur, so they are less likely to require medical input subsequently, and more likely to retain function. Patients may feel uncomfortable addressing some aspects of this approach, or worry that considering the psychology of pain implies that 'their pain is in their head'. This book explains that is not the case, but instead that pain is in some ways a bully, with no respect for age, gender, social status or any other marker of identity. Bullying does not exist in a single form. Physical bullying has psychological effects, and psychological bullying has physical consequences. Back pain is very much the same.

What is essential when patients are trying to recover from back pain is that they participate actively in the treatment plan and work with the treating team. What is set out in the pages that follow is a guide to how back pain arises, how it can be managed, and which symptoms are, and are not, worrying. Not everyone will benefit but those who read with an open mind, are honest with themselves, have realistic expectations, and engage with the approach are well placed to have a good chance of seeing their quality of life improve.

Perhaps the most important part – as with all treatments – is durability. Does any treatment last? The natural history of back pain is variable, and patients may be at risk of further exacerbations in future. Effective treatment therefore needs not only to address the current symptoms, but also to give patients the tools with which to manage their backs going forwards, both during good periods and during exacerbations of pain. The biopsychosocial approach has significant advantages over more medicalised treatments, such as surgery or injections; these are reactive, they are not appropriate early in the course of an episode, and patients may tend to relapse more quickly and be unable to self-manage effectively.

I commend this book to you to as a tool that may help now and will also be useful to refer back to in the future.

Mel Grainger FRCS (Orth)
Consultant spinal surgeon

# CHAPTER 1

# SHEDDING NEW LIGHT ON THE TREATMENT OF BACK PAIN

Most of us have experienced an episode of back pain at some point in our lives. More often than not it will settle within a few hours, or cause us trouble for a few days, then disappear without trace. Sometimes it may last for a few weeks, and we might consult a variety of healthcare professionals before, in time, the symptoms settle and life returns to normal. We may need to take some medication to help us for a short while, and we could be given lots of different explanations of why our backs hurt, but usually the pain does not make a significant difference to our quality of life in the long term.

However, you are probably reading this book because your back pain has persisted long beyond what you expected. It may be that those tried-and-tested treatments you took in the past, that previously worked so well, no longer help you. Back pain may have stopped you enjoying your interests or sport, or it might be preventing you from doing your usual job. You could even have withdrawn from social activities because you find it difficult to predict when you are going to have another bad day, so you've stopped making plans.

Living with unrelenting back pain depletes your physical and psychological resources; it can sap your wellbeing and deplete your strength and resilience. Having to cope with continual or frequently recurring back pain whilst dealing with the demands and difficulties of everyday life can feel overwhelming. Back pain – indeed, pain in any region of the body – demands our attention: this is what makes it such an effective signal. Pain usually acts as a protector: it makes us behave, move, and think differently to help the healing process. It can be so effective that it suspends thinking, feeling, or the ability to focus on anything else. And when it persists it can take over our lives.

*The good news is that research over the last few decades has produced a new way of viewing and treating low back pain – and it is having astounding results.*

### The cost of back pain

Back pain is one of the most common reasons for consulting a doctor, taking time off work or using medication. Back pain costs the European economies £12 billion per annum. It is the leading cause of long-term disability in the UK and is linked to other health complaints such as low mood, diabetes and heart disease. In terms of the global burden of disease, back pain was the most common cause of disability between 1990 and 2013. In short, it poses a huge burden on the individual, the health service and society as a whole and the economic costs to healthcare systems, industry and social-welfare support systems are phenomenal.

## A new model for treating back pain

Until recently persistent back pain was poorly understood. For many years the prevailing assumption was that all persistent back pain must be the result of structural abnormalities of the spine or joints. As in all traditional types of medical training, we were taught to look for a variety of structural abnormalities of the spine, most commonly arthritic and disc disorders, or for a vague group of conditions attributed to poor posture, under-exercise, over-exertion, worn-out tendons, and the like. Sometimes treatments that focused on these structural abnormalities worked, but far too frequently patients returned to the treatment room, frustrated with a further episode of pain, or unable to get rid of persistent back pain. There have been many different theories about which spinal structures are responsible for the pain, but none produced consistent results for people with persisting pain.

Over the past few decades a plausible biological and scientific model has emerged for working with people who suffer from persistent back pain and it is termed the 'biopsychosocial model'. The biopsychosocial model allows us to understand a person's experience of their pain in the context of their life, culture, hopes and aspirations, past experiences, thoughts, feelings and relationships, influenced by information gained both consciously and subconsciously from family, friends, media, and healthcare professionals. By exploring these social and psychological factors, we are able to identify aspects of patients' back pain experience that may be holding up their recovery.

At the same time, our knowledge of pain biology has improved immensely, through some detailed research done around the world by fantastic forward-thinking research teams. This has provided a new framework for helping us to understand better what happens biologically when pain in any part of the body persists, and the role that psychological and social factors play in determining how much pain we feel, how much disability we experience, and, most importantly, what can be done about it. This has helped researchers and clinicians establish new biopsychosocial approaches to treatment, which have shown promising results – results we have seen time and again at our own programme at the Royal Orthopaedic Hospital in Birmingham.

# Our journey

The way we examined and treated patients 20 years ago was a product of what we were taught at university and on post-graduate courses. Since then, we have dismissed much of it, as others' research combined with our own knowledge and experience has completely changed the way we view low back pain. Many brilliant clinicians and researchers were involved over the years in shaping a new approach, in which patients are encouraged to unlock their own 'pathways to recovery'. This idea was hugely influential on our own practice. It just seemed to make sense, and as we began to use it we realised that it worked.

Six years ago we were given the opportunity to set up a group-based treatment service at the Royal Orthopaedic Hospital in Birmingham, which would combine physical and psychological treatment principles to help people with persistent musculoskeletal pain, mostly back pain, return to the lives they had before. At the time, NHS guidelines recommended that such programmes should be a hundred hours long. Working in a climate of limited resources, we decided to explore whether a programme that followed the same principles but was much shorter could produce useful outcomes. We managed to persuade our local service commissioners that this service was worthy of the investment, and then set about structuring the service around a 12-hour, group-based treatment, which combined all the latest research on what works for people with persistent back pain. We managed to get funding so that both of us could be involved in the programme and, in time, we also gained funding for the services of a pain counsellor.

Using the structure of existing longer programmes, we established a service that addressed both the physical and psychological aspects of persisting back pain, and the social influences that influence the course of back pain: in other words, the biopsychosocial approach. We offered exercise and relaxation sessions, as well as helping patients to learn about and understand their back pain so that it no longer dominated their lives and their ability to function well. We looked at better ways to help them manage those difficult days and get the best out of medication. We both have experience in occupational health so were able, when needed, to guide people who were having difficulties in their chosen employment, or when aspects of their work were impacting on their health.

It is one thing making improvements in health and function at an appointment with a healthcare professional, but quite another to maintain that progress over time. We placed a lot of emphasis on changes that a person can make within their own environment and ways they can maintain momentum. Underpinning all of this we used a coaching-guiding method in which the person with the problem is viewed as having the resources, usually hidden, to get themselves better.

Pretty soon we recognised that for many people this approach was really working. We were seeing much better outcomes than we could ever have achieved with other treatment methods, such as physical manipulation or injection treatments, or just giving people sets of exercises to do. Using a team-based approach seemed to help them get back to activities they had previously enjoyed; their moods were lifting, they felt less anxious about using their backs for normal daily activities and they frequently reported that they were taking much less, or no medication and feeling better for doing so. Rather than simply being shown how to cope with back pain, people were telling us that they felt liberated from their back pain; that they felt much more in control of important areas of their lives and were in effect in the driving seat again. Moreover, they felt more confident dealing with the turbulent and difficult times encountered on life's journey, rather than these events 'flooring' them.

We think it is important for everyone to have an understanding of the principles we use on our programmes, and those used on other similar programmes, which can lead to a path of recovery. We are grateful that the publishers, Random House, have given us the opportunity to promote the benefits of this approach to a wider audience.

## Gavin's journey

Gavin Newman had spent years building up a career as a singer in pubs and clubs around the West Midlands. He loved singing and was overjoyed when he managed to make it his full-time job. He had a diary full of bookings and was finally enjoying the buzz of earning good money, doing something he had a real passion for. He specialised in singing the Rat Pack songs, such as 'Everybody Loves Somebody' by Dean Martin or 'New York, New York' by Frank Sinatra, and his routine was full of great material that had his audiences in raptures. He was living the dream and revelling in a world he had longed to be part of for many years. Life was good.

Then, one evening whilst singing on-stage, Gavin noticed a twinge in his back; nothing significant initially but as his set came towards the end, his back pain was increasing. He managed to get off stage but noticed the pain was continuing to worsen. Like most people who experience back pain, he thought it would be better by the morning, so he took himself to bed. The following morning, he woke early. He tried to move but felt an excruciating pain in his back; he felt locked, stuck, unsure what to do. Every time he tried to move he felt an overwhelming pain in his back. He couldn't even raise himself out of bed.

Pretty quickly Gavin started to feel alarmed. He had several more gigs booked over the next few days. 'How am I going to manage? I can't even move,' he worried. Somehow he managed to get himself out of bed but the pain continued unabated. This was a new experience for Gavin. He had never felt like this before and was sure there must be something seriously wrong. He cancelled the next couple of gigs, hoping to be fit after that but worried deep down that it might take much longer to recover.

Gavin went to see a doctor and was given some advice: 'Try to stay active and take these tablets. Don't worry; you will be fine in a few weeks. You will be back singing in no time.' But this didn't sit well with Gavin. He was sure there was something seriously wrong with his back, as it was so painful. He was anxious that his singing career, which he cherished so dearly, was in jeopardy; he was worried that he might do more damage to his back if he became more active. Within a few days Gavin started to feel depressed. Each time he went back to the doctor he was given the same message: 'Stay active, and you will be fine soon.' The doctor gave him more tablets, different tablets, some of which were stronger and some of which had unpleasant side-effects. Gavin kept following his doctor's advice but felt he was getting nowhere. He had to cancel the rest of his forthcoming gigs, and this started to hit him financially, adding to his worries. He was spiralling into a cycle of low mood, raised anxiety, distress and hopelessness at his predicament. He felt guilty that he was letting down everyone around him but couldn't see a way out.

Since he was failing to recover, his doctor decided to request an MRI scan of Gavin's back. Gavin had to wait several weeks to have this scan, in which time nothing changed. He was still struggling with normal daily activities, such as bending to put his socks on in the morning, walking to his local shop; even standing at the sink doing the washing-up was difficult. Refreshing sleep was non-existent so he was given more tablets to help with sleeping. By the time he had his scan, Gavin felt, in his words 'doped up to the eyeballs'.

He sat down with another doctor to hear his scan results and was told his discs were degenerating and bulging, and he might need surgery. Gavin felt devastated. 'How can I go from having a full-time singing career, with a diary full of bookings, some decent money coming in, to this?' he fretted. He started to worry about his long-term future. He wasn't keen on the idea of surgery, but he knew he wasn't getting any better. He was starting to feel lethargic and was losing his motivation. His dreams of a full-time singing career were in tatters. His doctor told him he couldn't give him any more tablets, as he was on the maximum dose of everything. Gavin felt desperate.

Something had to change.

Gavin was then referred to a doctor at a local hospital who worked in a treatment service that took a different view of Gavin's back pain. Up to this point, no one had explored the psychological effect Gavin's back pain was having on him, or the biology of what was happening in his body as this downward spiral had taken hold. No one had considered the social consequences of Gavin's back pain – the fact that he'd had to give up his singing career and the pleasure it gave him, and that he was suffering financially.

Gavin noticed this new doctor seemed different to the others he had seen. Although sceptical initially, he was reassured to be told that he could get better without surgery. This doctor asked different questions: he was interested in the experience Gavin was going through, the low mood, the anxiety, the uncertainty about the future, the impact the back pain was having on his ability to earn a wage. After gathering all this new information, the doctor examined Gavin's MRI scan then reassured him that it was safe to start moving, initially at simple levels, and that he wouldn't damage himself. This news was a revelation to Gavin. No one had told him he would not harm his back if he got moving. He had been convinced there was long-term damage that he would never recover from. His lack of progress, despite treatments he assumed would help, had reinforced the message that there must be serious damage.

The whole consultation with the new doctor was different. Gavin felt understood. His perception of what was wrong and how the future might look began to shift. He was also helped at this stage to understand that all the drugs he had been prescribed were, in fact, making him feel much worse and had become part of the problem. This, he could see for the first time, was within his ability to influence; this was something he might be able to take control of.

But Gavin remained sceptical that he could recover. 'Why should this work if nothing else has worked?' he asked. He had to test it out for himself. The doctor asked him to see a physiotherapist and to join a rehabilitation programme that would explore all the different factors that might be causing Gavin's back pain to persist. Sensing this was going to be different, Gavin went along on the first day. Lingering doubts persisted, though: 'How can they know what I'm feeling inside my body?' he thought. The first session was in a classroom, with a group of other people in a similar predicament. Gavin sat there, dismissive of the information he was being given. 'How can this possibly help me?' he wondered. He was then taken into a gymnasium and found himself lying on the floor, on an exercise mat, staring at the ceiling, as he was introduced to a relaxation exercise. 'What the heck am I doing here?' he questioned.

More challenging for Gavin was what came next. He was instructed to do some exercises: starting to stretch his spine, to bend and then to walk on a treadmill. All these activities filled him with dread. He felt anxious just seeing other people trying them. He could feel his heart beating faster, his palms were sweaty and he was agitated. He knew it would make him worse. But he gave it a go. He got on the treadmill and started walking. Much to his surprise he noticed that he didn't feel any worse. He managed six minutes. He then tried some other exercises and stretches, and although it hurt initially (which he was told to expect) he found he could do them without feeling worse. This was liberating for Gavin. For the first time in six months he got a sense he was starting to recover. His scepticism started to give way to optimism. This different approach was starting to reap benefits.

He learned that his ongoing pain wasn't due to his damaged discs but was linked to the fact that he had been avoiding activities he thought could damage him further, and had become fearful of moving his back too much. This, and several other factors, were adversely affecting his nervous system, which had become too sensitive, winding up his pain, and his body had gradually become deconditioned. This made sense to Gavin, particularly when it was mentioned that low mood, anxiety, fear, lack of sleep and worry could have a direct impact on how much pain he was feeling. None of these psychological factors, which had been a key part of Gavin's pain experience, had been addressed by any of the other health professionals he had seen, but they were one of the main reasons why his pain had persisted. He learned that if he started to build his activity in a step-by-step manner his function would improve, and he started to feel the benefits of relaxation exercises in helping to wind down his oversensitive nervous system.

As part of his recovery Gavin was encouraged to set some goals to work towards. Most of all he wanted to get off his tablets. With the support of his new doctor, he was encouraged to taper them off gradually over a period of a few weeks. As Gavin did this he noticed that the 'fogginess' he had experienced over the past few months was starting to lift. He started to be able to think more clearly and noticed that his sleep patterns improved.

The real Gavin was starting to emerge. He was taught what to do if he had another attack of back pain in the future, and every day he practised some breathing exercises he had been given. Although he was still feeling some back pain, within a few weeks Gavin had seen a dramatic improvement. He was exercising regularly, free from medication, and liberated from much of the anxiety, fear and caution that he had developed. Gavin felt his recovery was well on its way. He started looking forward to rebuilding his life.

CHAPTER 2

# WHAT IS PREVENTING YOUR RECOVERY?

For many years now we have been using the biopsychosocial model to work with people with persistent back pain and we have found that most report a significant improvement in function. They are able to return to their usual hobbies, social activities and responsibilities, caring for or nurturing others, or to their paid employment. They regularly tell us they have 'got a life again' and that family members have noticed positive changes in their health and wellbeing. Although they might still experience some back symptoms, these usually trouble them much less, and their function and quality of life is significantly enhanced.

In this book we will help you understand how you can apply a biopsychosocial model to help you unlock your pathway to recovery. Whilst it may take some time and perseverance, we now know that it gives you the best chance to restore function, reduce pain and improve your quality of life. So if you feel ready, let's get going.

## The biopsychosocial approach – what is it?

The biopsychosocial approach to back pain acknowledges that biological, psychological and social factors all play a role in your experience of back pain. You never get one without the others; they always link together. People with back pain are

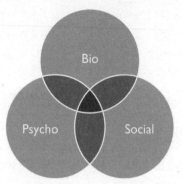

Figure 1 - The biopsychosocial approach in its simplest form.

much more likely to benefit from our treatment if we consider all three of these factors together, as in the story of Gavin earlier. Until fairly recently back pain treatment did not focus on such a broad view but it is now widely accepted that there is an association between psychological, biological and social factors whenever pain is experienced.

From a biological perspective we know that many changes occur in our bodies when we experience back pain: these involve our central nervous system (that is, the brain, spinal cord and the autonomic part of the nervous system – the part that controls internal functions such as heart rate, digestion and breathing); our endocrine system (governing the release of hormones); our immune system (which protects against disease); and our musculoskeletal system (muscles, tendons, bones and joints). These biological changes become more pronounced as back pain persists and play an important role in maintaining back pain and poor function long after we had expected to recover. We still don't fully understand all the myriad biological changes that occur when we experience back pain but researchers keep revealing new and exciting theories relating to the way these changes link to the pain experience. Learning about these can help you to recover.

From a psychological perspective, we know that when people experience an episode of back pain, there are a range of different responses. Some people become fearful of moving, and worry they might cause more damage to their back. Some avoid activity because they worry they may get a further disabling flare-up of back pain if they push themselves too much. These are normal and logical psychological responses to an episode of back pain, but if they persist unchecked they will contribute to ongoing back pain and poor function. Some people become overwhelmed with negative thoughts relating to their bad back and develop low mood or anxiety, just as Gavin did. They then get stuck in a vicious cycle of fear/avoidance/negativity which they struggle to recover from. It can be very difficult to break free of this cycle on your own but having an understanding of it will help.

From a social perspective, we know that the circumstances in which you live and work can influence your recovery. If people around you, including friends, family, work colleagues, health professionals or bosses, incorrectly view your back pain as a problem that means you need protecting or as something that could end your career, it will have a significant negative impact on your ability to recover. You might be influenced by stories in the media or online about back pain, but be aware that there is a lot of misinformation out there. These stories could be wrong, and following their advice could have the effect of prolonging your back pain and poor function rather than helping you to recover. Or you may be in a medical system that has long waiting lists, which means several months pass before you get the right advice about your back pain. By this point, many biological and psychological changes could have taken hold and you may find yourself in a cycle of persisting pain and poor function. Understanding how your social life links to your back pain will help you on the path to recovery.

To help yourself restore function and quality of life when back pain persists, it is helpful to understand how the biological, psychological and social systems all combine to maintain your pain problem. To start this process, let's explore the truth about persistent back pain.

## Key messages regarding persistent back pain

In our experience of working with persistent back pain, we come across many different and potentially conflicting opinions and nuggets of information people have been told about their back pain. They frequently attend our clinics with stories of what clinicians, friends, work colleagues and family members think is wrong with them. This advice has naturally influenced what they think and the way they react to their back pain but, while it was undoubtedly well-intentioned, it is often plain wrong.

It is important to understand the latest scientific evidence.

*As you read through the list below, take time to reflect on any differences between what you read here and what you currently believe and understand about your problem. It might be these differences are holding up your recovery.*

☞ In the majority of patients back pain is very difficult to diagnose

Despite numerous studies, it has become evident that diagnosing back pain is impossible in about 85% of patients. A very small percentage of people with persistent low back pain – estimates suggest less than 1% – have ongoing pain due to disease of the spine.

There are a number of different diseases affecting the spinal structures that might require medical treatment. These include the inflammatory diseases, some of which have complex medical names that sound scary – including rheumatoid arthritis, ankylosing spondylitis, or infections such as tuberculosis – but their symptoms can be very similar to other more benign conditions. Cancer can affect the spine and untreated will lead to rapid deterioration of health. Some people may have curvatures of their spine sufficiently advanced to affect the functioning of their internal organs, but it is worth mentioning that small curvatures of the spine are remarkably common and harmless although they seem to get the blame for a lot of back pain.

Remember that the vast majority of people with back pain have *no* identifiable underlying disease. This type of back pain is often referred to as 'non-specific'. Spending time and energy trying to find the specific structure in your spine that is causing pain is often a fruitless exercise. It is now widely acknowledged in healthcare circles that instead of trying to identify and diagnose what is responsible for your pain, it is more helpful to concentrate on using active approaches, such as those described in the chapters of this book, to help to restore function and quality of life and to minimise the effects of ongoing symptoms.

☞ MRI scans are useful if you have serious disease in your spine

People with any symptoms of biomedical diseases of the spine, such as those listed in the Red Flags box below, require investigations. MRI scans, X-rays and blood tests are commonly used. The advent of Magnetic Resonance Imaging (MRI) provided the opportunity to look at the structure of the back in great detail. For the first time, we were able to view bones, discs, nerves and spinal joints. These scans are without any doubt really effective in identifying *serious* spinal disease: for example, cancer, an infection or compression of the spinal cord. Using MRIs, surgeons are able to build a visual picture of the structure of the spine prior to surgery, and can perform detailed, precise operations when required as part of the treatment for that specific condition. The days of surgeons performing 'exploratory operations' on the spine are long gone, due to these advances. At the Royal Orthopaedic Hospital in Birmingham, as no doubt in all similar spinal services, we have frequent case conferences with our surgical colleagues if there is any doubt about the need for surgical or other invasive treatment.

## Red Flags

Talk to your GP if you experience any of the following:

- Ongoing back pain following a violent injury – for example a fall downstairs or a fall from a height
- Back pain which has got progressively worse week by week
- A previous history of cancer, drug abuse, HIV or long-term steroid use
- You feel generally unwell, have an ongoing high temperature, or have lost weight for no clear reason
- Your spine has developed a very obvious unusual shape which has not corrected itself over several months
- You are unable to control your bladder or bowel at all or you feel numb in this area
- You have pins and needles, numbness or weakness in both arms or both legs
- Your back is stiff for several hours in the morning
- Your walking pattern has become unsteady or uncoordinated
- Your back pain is much worse at night

☞ MRI scans which show structural changes to the spine such as 'wear and tear' and 'bulging discs' are common in people without back pain

Until recently, it was commonly assumed that persistent low back pain was due to changes to the structure of the spine, such as degenerating discs (wear and tear) and bulging discs (slipped discs). This formed the basis of the biomedical approach. For many years, it was believed that these spinal changes were the main reason for back pain and limited function. After MRI scans, people were often given very negative messages and labels regarding their spine. Diagnoses such as 'wear and tear', 'worn out', 'slipped discs', 'cracked discs', 'bulging discs' and 'degeneration' usually generate anxiety or feelings of helplessness – feelings that lead to extra caution when using the back for daily activities.

It may surprise you to know that research into MRI scans and back pain has found that the changes described above are just as common in people who have never experienced a significant episode of back pain. For example, 90% of people in their 60s who have never experienced a bad bout of back pain will have degenerating discs; more than 50% of people in their 40s who have never experienced a bad bout of back pain will have disc bulges; and 30% of people in their 20s who have never experienced back pain will have disc protrusions (large disc bulges). These changes become more common as people get older but there is enormous variation between individuals within the same age group.

In our work we regularly see people who suffer greatly with persistent back pain, yet when we look at MRI scans of their spines, there is no evidence of degenerating or bulging discs. Conversely, we can see patients make tremendous progress with rehabilitation in spite of alarming-looking degenerating and bulging discs on their MRI scans.

Given the fact that many people who have persistent back pain undergo MRI scans and X-rays as part of their management of back pain, we feel it is essential that you understand that many common findings on an MRI scan are just as likely to be found in people who have never had an episode of back pain. In short, the link between common spinal changes as identified on MRI or X-ray in the back and persisting back pain and poor function is weak. So whilst current understanding acknowledges that changes such as degenerating discs can *contribute* to persisting back pain and poor function, they do not tell us the whole story about why back pain persists.

☞ When back pain persists it is unlikely to be due to damage to the structures in your back

Damage to the important structures of the back is a rare event. High-speed road collisions, falls downstairs and serious assaults can result in spinal fractures that may require spinal surgery or a period of immobilisation. Occasionally disc bulges can compress the important nerves in your back and cause weakness in your legs, but these events are not commonplace. Some serious diseases such as cancer can also cause damage to the back, which may need the attention and skills of a spinal surgeon. But most of the time, back pain is not due to damage to the tissues in your back – even though it might feel as if they are damaged.

It is important to understand this, because researchers have found that if people are worried about perceived damage to their back, or fearful about causing further damage, they struggle to function as well as someone without these fears. It therefore becomes a factor preventing recovery. Usually anxiety about damage is not based on any hard scientific facts but is driven by underlying fear, which has the effect of maintaining pain.

☛ Persistent back pain affects your mood, which can delay or prevent recovery

Many people we work with tell us that they avoid activities they previously enjoyed, such as walking, going to the gym, playing table tennis, doing the garden or going to the cinema, for fear of causing further damage. This affects their mood and self-confidence over a period of time and their quality of life can be seriously affected. Sometimes they are unable to earn a living, leading to financial worries, possible relationship difficulties, and a sense of loss. They may find themselves becoming more anxious about the future and fretting over things that would not normally bother them. People report becoming more irritable than usual and tell us they find it difficult to relax. Sleep quality deteriorates. Ongoing distress linked to back pain will prolong their suffering and delay or even prevent recovery.

But all this can be reversed with the right approach.

It is really important to understand that activity is unlikely to cause any damage to your spine if you have persistent back pain. In chapter 6, you'll find advice about managing your daily activity and throughout the book you will learn new ways of dealing with ongoing distress.

☞ **The way people around you respond to your back pain can influence your recovery**

Your family, employers and the social circle around you are key to your recovery when back pain persists. If others over-protect you and do everything for you, making you feel as if you are made of fragile glass, it will prevent your recovery. Their reactions are understandable; they are trying to be helpful and have the best of intentions, but they are misguided. If you do not get the chance to test what your back can manage, you won't realise that increasing activity step by step is the best path to recovery. Those who understand that you are experiencing difficulties but still allow you to get on with things at your own pace are the most helpful.

Do remember, however, that those around you are not mind-readers. You have to let them know from time to time what difficulties you are experiencing and how you are feeling about things. Ask for any help you do need and explain how long you might need it for, making your request as specific as possible.

☞ **Believing it is someone else's job to fix your back will prevent recovery**

People with persistent back pain who take control of their own recovery, and follow advice such as that described in this book, have a much better chance of regaining function and quality of life. Conversely, if you believe there is a quick fix for your back, and that it is someone else's job to sort you out, it is likely the recovery won't happen. The general consensus from research is that active self-management approaches give you the best chance to restore function and quality of life when back pain persists.

☞ Accepting your back pain, and focusing less on trying to get rid of it, will help you recover

When back pain persists for longer than a few months, and you have tried several different treatments with limited benefit, you may have to accept that you won't be able to get rid of it completely. Whilst this may seem depressing, researchers have identified that if you focus less on getting rid of your pain, and more on getting back to activities that give meaning and purpose in your life, you are likely to have improved quality of life, you are likely to function better, you are likely to have better mental health and, curiously, you are likely to feel less pain. Accepting some level of pain, and the feelings, thoughts and emotions that go with it, rather than fighting it and getting angry about it, can be really helpful and can boost your recovery.

☞ Unresolved conflict in any aspect of your life can prevent recovery

When the onset of pain is associated with an accident, perhaps at work or on the road, it can lead to a sense of victimhood; someone else is to blame and must be made to pay for the suffering you have endured. These feelings are understandable but the sense of injustice feeds rage and feelings of helplessness into the nervous system, which are guaranteed to make your pain worse and prevent recovery.

Other life stressors such as relationship problems, debt and family conflict can also impact on your pain. In chapter 12, we look at ways of addressing the stress in your life.

It's important to recognise you have a choice here, as with everything else: how you choose to respond to the misfortunes that life gives you makes a big difference to what happens to you.

☞ Staying in work, whether it is paid or voluntary, is likely to help your back

It is common for back pain to affect your ability to work. To clarify, by 'work' we mean some meaningful or purposeful activity in your life, either paid or voluntary, including caregiving roles; our definition is by no means restricted to sitting at a desk in an office. Established research shows that people with some type of purposeful role in life experience fewer problems with daily activities. There is more about managing your working life in chapter 11.

☞ The phrase 'psychosocial factors' does not mean the pain is all in your head!

One common misunderstanding when we talk about psychological and social factors is to think we are suggesting the pain is imaginary. Quite the contrary! However, psychological factors are very logical and natural responses to an episode of back pain. It is natural to become more vigilant and anxious when we experience pain, and accordingly to reduce activity and increase rest. This is a logical way to respond, allowing tissues to heal and the body to recover. However, when back pain persists even though the tissues have healed, people frequently become scared of moving again. This fear of movement often takes hold and can set up a cycle of inactivity, low mood, loss of confidence and anxiety about returning to normal leisure pursuits and work activities. Having a better understanding of how these psychosocial factors impact on recovery gives you more choices and will allow you to take positive steps towards recovery.

☛ Some medications taken for back pain can be unhelpful in the long run

One of the mainstays of treatment for persistent back pain is medication. It can be beneficial in order to help get you moving but some medications, both those purchased over the counter and prescribed by medical practitioners, can be counter-productive and make recovery more difficult. Understanding how to get the best out of medication, and being aware of the potential pitfalls, is a key component of unlocking your pathway to recovery. There is more about medication in chapter 7.

☛ Familiar flare-ups in back pain are not due to damage to the spine

When we experience a bad flare-up in back pain it is frequently overwhelming. People regularly report that it feels as if something has been damaged within the structure of the back. They feel helpless and desperate for a solution. It ruins plans for holidays, weekends away or nights out, and sometimes lasts for days or even weeks. However, most of the time flare-ups in back pain are not due to damage – especially if it is a familiar pain – and can be resolved quickly and effectively, with a few simple techniques.

Flare-ups in back pain can consume our every waking thought for hours or even days. Researchers have discovered that those who have very catastrophic, negative thoughts when they experience a sudden flare-up in back pain will take longer to recover than those who have a clear and logical plan for recovery. So, surprisingly, recovery from a flare-up is less to do with how much pain you feel at the time than with what you think about the flare-up, and what you do about it.

Because it feels as if something must be damaged in our backs, we naturally become more cautious as, consciously or subconsciously, we live in fear of another relapse. This can be a factor preventing recovery. Taking back a degree of control over flare-ups of back pain is very empowering and will give a huge boost to your confidence. In chapter 10 we help you to understand the factors that make flare-ups more likely and to create your own plan for recovery from a flare-up.

## Persistent back pain and human biology

One of the key changes in clinical practice in recent years has been the way we view persistent pain. Instead of focusing on the structures of the back, such as discs, joints and bones, research has helped us to understand that ongoing persistent pain has much more to do with biological changes in the nervous system (from the tip of our toes to the top of our brain), endocrine system and immune system, than in the structures of the spine. For example, we now know that the very real physical examination findings we notice in patients with persistent back pain reflect biological changes in the nervous system; the affected muscles are in a continual state of cramp or excessive tone and the nervous system has become sensitised.

It is clear that many of the psychosocial factors described above are linked to changes in the nervous system, endocrine system and immune system and are directly related to the amount of pain you feel and how well you are able to function. So, having a better understanding of psychological and social factors and how they link to your body's biology when you have persistent back pain is an essential part of helping you to restore function and quality of life. That is why we place great emphasis in this book on explaining the biology of pain and how it links to psychological and social factors.

In the next chapter we will explore what is happening in your body from a biological perspective when back pain persists.

# CHAPTER 3

# THE DANGER-ALERT SYSTEM

We explained in the previous chapter that our beliefs about what actually causes back pain have changed. We have moved away from the assumption that all back pain is due to structural changes in the spine such as slipped discs, degenerated discs or joints being out of place. We know that these structures can contribute to the overall experience of back pain, but more recent theories based on scientific research into how our brain and nervous system function have helped us to understand that ongoing persistent pain in any region of the body has more to do with changes in the nervous system and how we respond to these changes.

To begin with, we need to define what pain is. The formal definition developed by the International Association for the Study of Pain states: 'Pain is an unpleasant sensory and emotional experience associated with actual or potential tissue damage or described in terms of such damage.' This definition makes it clear that pain is an unpleasant experience with both sensory *and* emotional aspects – not either/or – and that it is associated with perceived or actual damage to the body. People we see with persistent back pain often tell us that it does really feel as if something important is damaged.

To help clarify this definition, let's think of what happens when we sprain our ankle. We nearly always feel an initial sharp pain as we go over on our ankle. Sometimes it will look swollen, sometimes it will feel hot, and it may appear red. These are signs of actual damage to the ankle region. It will usually take a few weeks to settle as the tissues heal. We may limp for a while and we may watch the physical appearance of our ankle change as the tissues heal. Sometimes, though, when we sprain our ankle it will hurt just as much initially, but it won't look swollen, it won't feel hot and it won't look red. We will perceive damage, but frequently there *is* no damage and the ankle will return to normal within a few minutes or hours. Although it felt as if we had damaged the tissues, we actually hadn't.

These two experiences feel the same, but in one instance there is tissue damage whilst in the other instance there is no damage. This is frequently the case with back pain, particularly sudden flare-ups in pain. Although it feels as if we have damaged our back, this is usually not the case.

So, when we experience pain, sometimes it is because we have damaged part of our body, but just as commonly there is no damage. It is important to understand this before we look at why pain persists later on in this chapter.

## Types of pain

It is generally accepted that there are two different types of pain: acute pain and persistent (or chronic) pain.

### Acute pain

Acute pain is pain of recent origin; for example, the sudden pain you feel when you bang your knee or hit your head on a shelf. It immediately alerts you to a threat of damage to some part of your body so that you can take appropriate action to avoid repetition, take steps to heal the injured area and thus enhance your chances of survival. It is a useful alarm signal to tell us there is something wrong in the part of the body that hurts, and that we need to pay attention and do something about it. Healing will take different amounts of time, depending on what we have damaged. Skin is quickest to heal, usually within a few days, but bones can take several weeks or even a few months to heal. Muscles and ligaments will typically heal within a few weeks but some of the larger tendons can take longer than bones to heal.

The important thing to note here is that acute pain is necessary for healing and recovery, when tissues of our body are damaged. It serves a highly useful purpose in telling us to protect an injured area whilst healing takes place. Once the area has healed, the pain settles and we can return to normal.

This type of pain is really useful. If we didn't know we had hurt a part of our body, and were not alerted to it, we might carry on with activity regardless and our body might not be able to heal itself. So acute pain serves as a useful protective device to alert us that part of our body is in danger and might need protecting in order to heal.

## Persistent or chronic pain

Persistent pain, including persistent back pain, is biologically very different to acute tissue injury pain. It is generally accepted that any pain that has lasted for more than three or four months can be described as persistent or chronic. For the purposes of this book, we will call it persistent pain.

Persistent pain is no longer useful to us for immediate survival. It is pain that has persisted long after the tissues of the body have healed and is more associated with the nervous system. If you are reading this book because you have persistent back pain, it is important to understand that when back pain persists, it is not due to a failed healing process, since any 'injured' tissues have healed as figure 2 illustrates.

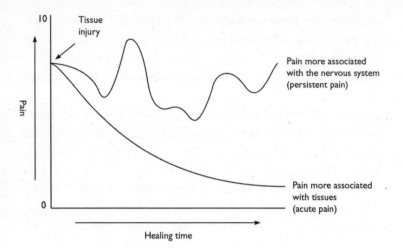

Figure 2 – The difference between acute and persistent pain (adapted from Moseley and Butler, *Explain Pain*, NOI Group).

Persistent pain can really drag you down. It can make you feel fed up, angry, annoyed and frustrated. It can vary from day to day. On some days you might feel as if you are over the worst of it, whilst on other days it feels as if you can't even raise yourself out of bed. It doesn't follow a consistent pattern in the way acute pain does, and will sometimes feel as if it will never go away. Whilst it is relatively easy to predict when your recovery will be complete with acute pain, this is not the case with persistent pain.

It is still common for healthcare professionals to hunt around looking for damaged tissues long after healing is completed, in a vain effort to explain persistent pain. You may have experienced this yourself during your journey with back pain. But we now know that persisting pain has more to do with biological changes in our nervous system, how we respond to those changes, and what we think about our pain, than actual ongoing injury or damage in the body. These biological changes and our psychological response to these changes and the social context in which we exist can turn up the volume in our nervous system, like an amplifier pumping out loud music.

*As long as these changes continue, the pain persists.*

Figure 3 – Persistent pain can be due to many different biological, psychological and social factors. These factors can turn the volume up on your pain.

## The 'danger-alert' system

It is important to understand that all pain we experience is a response from a specific part of our nervous system – the danger-alert system. This system, which exists to protect us from harm, is constantly detecting the tiniest changes in the body and telling the brain about them. The danger-alert system is part of a highly sophisticated system of nerve fibres called neurones, which contain sensors that are present in all our body's tissues. They are constantly sniffing and sampling the local environment for activity that might be threatening. These sensors have evolved to be quite specialised. Some respond to temperature changes, such as when we touch a warm radiator or step under a cold shower. Some will respond to mechanical forces, such as when our shoes feel too tight. Others respond to the presence of chemical changes, such as when we feel a burning sensation in our muscles after vigorous exercise, caused by a build-up of lactic acid.

Neurones link our sensors to the spinal cord, where they link in to our central nervous system. They are constantly sending information into our spinal cord. If you are sitting down as you read this book, you can probably feel the mechanical receptors working in your thighs and buttocks, as the pressure of sitting will activate them.

Sometimes, these sensors will be activated quite strongly, such as when we touch a roasting hot oven, or step on something sharp. At those moments the sensors will send a larger volley of signals towards the central nervous system. If the signals are strong enough, they will activate other nerves, which then fire a 'danger-alert' message to the spinal cord. You need to know pretty quickly that something dangerous might be happening in your body's tissues. Activity of this type in these neurones is called 'nociception', which literally means 'danger reception'. These sensors are your first protection against potential harm. They amplify the message if the volley

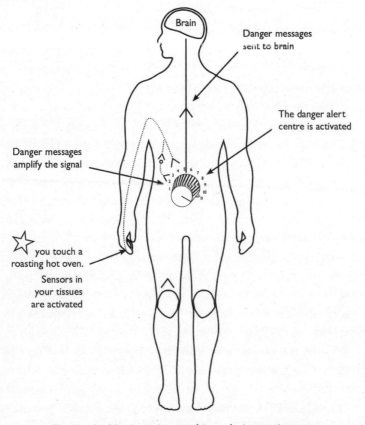

Figure 4 - Nociception and its role in turning up
our danger-alert system when we touch a hot oven.

of signals reaches a certain intensity, just like turning up the volume on your television with your remote control.

So the spinal cord is always receiving messages from your sensors and sometimes these messages are danger messages. To take this a stage further, the processing centre in the spinal cord that receives these messages is constantly communicating to the brain. Figure 4 shows how this happens.

## Assessing different levels of threat

When your brain receives danger-alert messages from the spinal cord it has to ask itself a few questions to make sense of all the incoming information.

- 'Have I experienced these danger sensations before?'
- 'Where are they coming from?'
- 'Are these danger-alert sensations a threat to survival?'
- 'What should I do about them?'

The brain does this in an amazingly complex way, in an instant, without us being conscious of it. It needs to check if all this new information is familiar and not a threat, or whether it is something new, uncertain, and potentially life-threatening.

If the brain computes that these incoming sensations are or could be a threat to us, it activates another group of neurones, which communicate between the brain and the spinal cord. These neurones have the ability to turn up danger-alert messages from the brain to the spinal cord. Once this happens, pain is likely to be experienced. It alerts us to danger, and motivates us to take action. We then have to decide what is the best thing to do. The really important thing to understand is that the amount of traffic travelling along this group of neurones is governed by the degree of threat the brain perceives we are facing.

All living creatures with a central nervous system have this brain function; it is vital for survival, as it helps to protect them from danger. This function is rather similar to highly trained guards, whose duty is to protect a highly valuable establishment when a threat is perceived.

Reflect on Gavin's story, which we told back in chapter 1. He had never experienced back pain before. The danger-alert messages from his back to his spinal cord to his brain were very unfamiliar and alarming. Because his brain could not find a previous memory of back pain in its archives, it decided that these new sensations were a major threat. All Gavin's attention was drawn towards these danger-alert messages, motivating him to take action and do something about them.

Consider how much threat his back pain caused him: threat of loss of income, threat of loss of status as a singer, threat of losing work, threat of not knowing whether he would recover, threat of not knowing what was going on in his back, threat of loss of control, and more. His guard room was overworking, never resting, turning up his danger-alert system so loud that he couldn't think of anything else. All of these threats ultimately overwhelmed him and as long as his brain kept computing that the sensations were a threat, his pain continued to persist and quickly engulfed him. He did not yet know all the key messages we looked at in chapter 2, adding to his sense of ongoing threat, thus winding up his danger-alert system. 'Am I damaging myself? Have I slipped a disc? What does the future hold for me now?' he panicked. Figure 5 explains the process.

| Common threats related to back pain |
| --- |
| Being anxious about whether you will be able to work with your bad back |
| Worrying that your back pain will get worse as you get older |
| Uncertainty about whether you will ever get better |
| Fear of causing more damage to your back |
| Frustration that you can't get back to normal |
| Anger that prescribed treatments don't seem to work |
| Feeling dismissed by healthcare professionals |

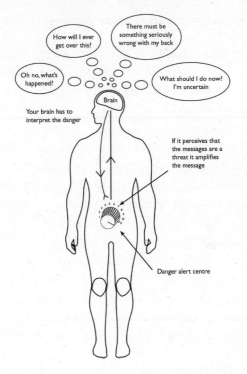

Figure 5 – The brain turns up the danger-alert system.

Some of the more common threats that people tell us about their back pain experience are summarised in the box above. You may be able to add some others from your own experience. All of them will maintain the threat associated with back pain and will be responsible for maintaining the danger-alert messages, and thus the pain.

From a biological perspective all the neurones within our nervous system communicate with each other by releasing chemical messengers that have evolved for specific functions. The chemical messengers associated with turning up the volume in our nervous system include adrenaline and cortisol, the exact same chemicals as those associated with our danger-alert system. We will explain how this might impact on your back pain in the next chapter, because understanding this could help to unlock your pathway to recovery.

## Turning down the danger-alert system

The nervous system can turn up the danger messages through-out your body, including in your back. The good news is that it can also turn *down* the danger messages.

You can probably think of things you do to ease the discom-fort when your back hurts. Typically, you might rub or massage it. In doing this, you stimulate other sensors connected to neu-rones in your body's tissues, which send volleys of messages to the spinal cord. Again, If the signals are strong enough, they will activate other neurones, which will turn down the volume of the danger-alert message in the spinal cord.

You can see this in action if you watch a footballer get hurt in a tackle. He might appear to be in agony until the physi-otherapist runs onto the pitch and attends to him. In many cases, out of sight, something magic seems to happen: the player quickly gets up and continues playing. The magic ingre-dient could be a cold spray applied to the area that hurts. By using this, the physiotherapist is stimulating sensors that send messages along specific neurones to turn down the danger-alert signals. Once they do this, it is likely that less pain is experienced.

Parents do this instinctively. When they see their child fall and hurt his or her knee, without even thinking about it they start rubbing the sore knee, thus calming the danger-alert mes-sages, and pretty soon the pain eases. Figure 6 explains how this works.

*In the same way that nature has given us a pathway from the brain to the spinal cord to turn up the danger-alert messages, there are also pathways from the brain to the spinal cord that have evolved to turn down the danger-alert messages.*

This is a very complex system but essentially if the brain com-putes that the incoming sensations from the spinal cord are not threatening or alarming, it will activate neurones that have the

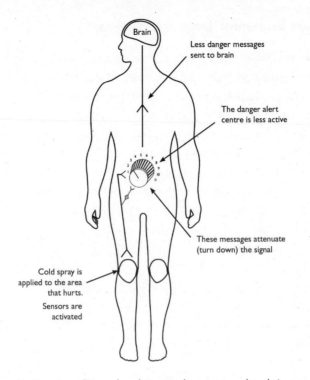

Figure 6 – Turning down the danger-alert system by doing something soothing to the area that hurts.

ability to turn down danger-alert messages from the brain to the spinal cord. We can then continue with whatever we are doing, without the need to take any further action. Returning to Gavin's story, by reassuring him that his back wasn't seriously damaged, that it was safe for him to get moving if he did it step by step, that movement would not cause a bad flare-up in his pain, and that he could recover, he started to feel less threatened by his pain. Once he understood the key messages regarding back pain that we detailed in chapter 2, he started to notice he was recovering, despite having had ongoing back pain for many months.

Again, the really important thing to understand is that the amount of traffic travelling along this group of neurones is governed by the degree of threat the brain perceives.

## Nature's inherent analgesic pathway

There are lots of things you can do that will start to send more traffic down this pathway, which we like to refer to as nature's inherent analgesic pathway – a natural way of easing pain. This is the key to your pathway to recovery. We aim to teach you these skills throughout the book in order to promote your recovery. Figure 7 illustrates how it works.

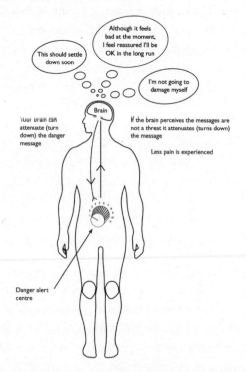

Figure 7 – The role of the brain in turning down the danger-alert system.

If we return to the example of the physiotherapist attending to the injured player, what you can't see happening from the sidelines is that the physiotherapist is talking to the player and, where appropriate, reassuring him that it is safe to continue. This is also what mothers do when their child is hurt. They are both reassuring and distracting the person in pain at the same time, which sends traffic down nature's inherent analgesic pathway from the brain to the danger-alert processing centre in the spinal cord.

During his time on the rehabilitation programme Gavin discovered for himself the benefits of accessing nature's inherent analgesic pathway. He had previously felt very threatened by his back pain, and upset about the impact it was having on his life. He had become very anxious and fearful about doing too much and thus causing another flare-up of his pain. This was keeping his danger-alert centre highly activated. But he learned breathing and relaxation exercises, gentle spinal stretches and graded exercise strategies. He set goals for himself, which he achieved and was helped to overcome his anxiety. All of this reduced the threat associated with his back pain, sending traffic from his brain down nature's inherent analgesic pathway. And we know that the more these pathways are used, the stronger they get.

Some examples of activities, thoughts and feelings that promote the strengthening of nature's inherent analgesic pathway are listed below. Try to think of some that you can add for yourself.

| Activities that strengthen the analgesic pathway |
| --- |
| Getting back to hobbies or interests we previously enjoyed |
| Learning relaxation techniques |
| Feeling valued within our social group |
| Fun and laughter with close friends and family |
| Returning to exercise |
| Returning to work |
| Setting goals and achieving them |
| Building up a healthy social life |

The neural pathways between the brain and spinal cord that turn down danger-alert messages communicate at a biological level by the release of specific chemical messengers, such as endorphins and serotonin. These chemical messengers are part of the mind-body reward system. Every time we engage in pleasurable activities, we are helping to give ourselves a small dose of 'feel-good' chemicals. We will look at ways in which you can activate these yourself in the following chapters.

## The pain-gate system

The modern understanding of pain biology was introduced to us in the 1960s by two renowned neuroscientists, Dr Ronald Melzack and Dr Patrick Wall. They developed the gate-control theory of pain, utilising the metaphor of the opening and closing of a gate. If the gate is open more pain is experienced. This theory has been developed further by many other neuroscience researchers, including more recently Dr Lorimer Moseley who helped us to understand the role of the danger-alert system in understanding pain, as described above. The key message from all of this work is this:

*Our brain has the capacity to influence the amount of pain we feel, and we all have the ability to control this, no matter which parts of our bodies might be hurting – including our backs.*

The pain-gate system helps to explain those well-documented events in which humans were subjected to massive trauma yet somehow could persevere without feeling any pain, at least initially.

This much broader view of pain allows us to treat people with back pain using a different model, which incorporates the biopsychosocial approach. Making several small changes across different aspects of your day-to-day life will make a huge difference overall to your level of pain and ability to function. Later chapters will look at this in more detail.

You may have heard of the marginal gains approach used to improve performance in business and sport. A term coined by Sir David Brailsford, who was director of the highly successful

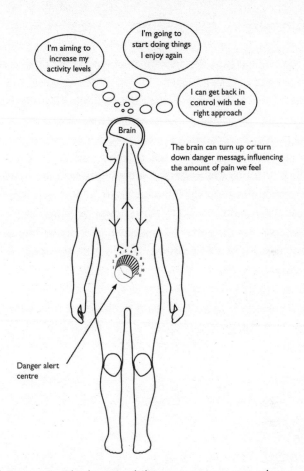

Figure 8 - The brain's ability to turn up or turn down
our danger-alert system.

British cycling team that won so many medals at two Olympic games and managed the team that won the Tour de France twice, it means that small incremental gains will eventually add up to a huge overall improvement. You can use the principles of a marginal gains approach to make a success of your own recovery. Making a number of small changes in different areas of your life, using the principles described in this book, will all add up together. This approach is far more likely to be successful than looking for a solution from one source only.

## In summary

- Evolution has provided us with an inherent danger-alert system to protect us from harm.
- The brain has to make sense of the danger-alert messages coming in and, if it computes with all the information available from memory, experience or context that you are in a threatening situation, then pain will be produced.
- The pain is there to attract our attention to the perceived threat. Understanding why the brain has come to this conclusion is the key to liberating yourself from persistent back pain.
- The brain has the ability to turn down danger-alert messages, and learning how to do this yourself is likely to promote recovery.

The key messages about back pain in chapter 2 may have helped you to start this process, but there is more to come.

# CHAPTER 4

# UNDERSTANDING WHY YOUR PAIN PERSISTS

Before we look at how you can help yourself to recover, it is helpful to understand the biological processes that cause us to feel persistent pain, wherever we experience it in our bodies. This chapter is designed to provide you with a fresh understanding of what may be happening in your body. It will also help you to understand how these biological processes link to the psychological and social factors we discussed earlier. Once you understand your pain from all these perspectives you may be able to identify what is preventing you from recovering function and quality of life.

As explained in chapter 3, our danger-alert system has evolved over millions of years, and is one of the key criteria governing whether we feel pain or not. When our danger-alert system is switched on, it will also switch on what is known as the fight, flight or freeze arousal system. If you have ever been driving late at night and come upon a rabbit on the road ahead, you will have seen this in action. Hopefully the rabbit will run away, as its 'flight' response kicks in, but sometimes they 'freeze' instead, dazzled by the headlights.

Consider the meerkat grazing in the savannah. It is relaxed until it begins to sense vibration coming through the ground and getting closer. Within an instant it is alert to danger, standing on its hind legs, surveying the world, with eyes wide open, ears pricked up, muscles ready and prepared to run. Its senses are primed to alert it to anything dangerous because its survival is at stake. Humans are the same.

This fight-flight-freeze system works through our autonomic (automatic) nervous system, which releases adrenaline, cortisol and other chemical messengers into the bloodstream. All of this activity ramps up the nervous system for intense activity, to energise it to fight, fly or freeze. Gavin's responses to his back pain – agitation, sweaty palms and rapid heartbeat – were all due to activity in his autonomic nervous system. This comprises two separate systems – the sympathetic and the parasympathetic, and it's worth understanding a little more clearly what each of them does.

## The sympathetic nervous system

This is a very powerful automatic system that responds rapidly to any threatening situation, allowing you to act quickly and powerfully if required. If your brain perceives any threat around you, it will fire up this system, and release adrenaline from the adrenal gland, above the kidney. Adrenaline is highly effective at helping us to narrow our focus onto the threat, while another chemical called cortisol makes oxygen available to the brain, muscles and heart to prepare us for action. We will feel the physical effect of this immediately, as our heart will beat faster, our palms will become sweaty, sometimes hairs stand on end, and we will feel agitated.

This response can be very helpful in the short term as it allows your brain to decide whether to fight, fly or freeze in response to the threat it has detected. This system was highly advantageous for our ancestors as it helped them to escape from predators. Remember, it is all entirely automated; there is no time for thinking in an emergency situation.

The sympathetic nervous system can be switched on very quickly, and will usually return to normal within a short space of time, usually a few minutes. Some people love the buzz of adrenaline in their system and are attracted to activities that give this buzz, such as sky diving or off-piste skiing. Those who are prone to excessive outbursts of anger might, without realising it, be addicted to the buzz of adrenaline that getting angry gives them. It is stimulated by rapid, often shallow, breathing where the in-breath is longer than the out-breath, a common habit among people who are prone to anxiety. This habitual pattern of breathing, so often unrecognised by the individual, also increases tension in the muscles at the front of the neck and can lead to chronic pain around the neck and shoulders.

Whilst this system is really helpful in the short term, to alert us to potential danger, if it remains switched on it can contribute to persisting pain by raising and maintaining muscle tension. Persistent pain and stress are usually associated with persistently increased levels of adrenaline. Adrenaline does not cause pain by itself, but when there is a heightened danger-alert sensitivity sending messages to the brain, adrenaline can magnify that danger message and increase the level of pain.

## The parasympathetic nervous system

The parasympathetic nervous system is concerned with calming, slowing and conserving energy. It is more active during refreshing sleep, meditation and rest. It is stimulated directly by slowing down the rate of breathing, especially making the out-breath longer than the in-breath. We teach this pattern of breathing to our patients early on in their treatment and in chapter 9 we will explain how to do it. When people who have been in pain for a long time start to practise the method, they report dramatic improvements in their comfort and sleep patterns. The parasympathetic system may therefore help you to unlock your pathway to recovery.

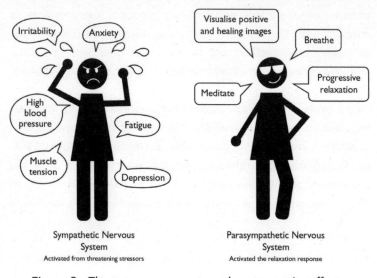

Figure 9 – The two nervous systems have opposite effects.

## The nervous system and back pain

Armed with this knowledge about the fight-flight-freeze system, let's consider what happens in an acute back pain episode.

Usually a triggering event fires off the body's fight, flight and freeze mechanism and the result can be intense muscle cramp. People sometimes tell us that they feel lopsided. Muscles on one side of their body might be contracting more than on the other, which will have the effect of pulling joints out of alignment because these muscles can have a phenomenal grip. The body is in an effective 'freeze' and a huge amount of energy is diverted to maintaining the cramping muscles. While the fight, flight and freeze mechanism remains switched on the muscles stay contracted for prolonged periods of time and eventually become starved of oxygen.

Lack of oxygen supply to a tissue is called ischaemia; it hurts, as we start to produce lactic acid in the muscle. This then activates those neurones that have evolved to fire danger signals when chemical changes are detected. This creates a perfect vicious cycle as the spinal cord is bombarded with danger messages from the tissues and these continue to activate and maintain the fight-flight-freeze reaction.

So the fight, flight and freeze response is a key component of those overwhelming episodes of back pain you may experience from time to time, resulting in significant, overwhelming muscle cramps. Understanding this at a biological level is key to helping you unlock your pathway to recovery when back pain persists. In later chapters we will return to this to show you what you can do about it.

We have other systems that will also kick into action when the danger-alert system is switched on, including the endocrine system and the immune system.

## The endocrine system

The endocrine system comprises a number of glands, including the pituitary and hypothalamus in the brain and the adrenal glands, which sit above the kidneys. These produce hormones that regulate all aspects of our body function. When our danger-alert system is switched on, either by sensors in our body's tissues or by our brains perceiving a threatening situation, the hypothalamus releases hormones, which in turn make the pituitary gland releases hormones into the bloodstream. The adrenal gland then recognises that these hormones are in the bloodstream and cortisol is released. This all happens within a few minutes.

Unlike the sympathetic nervous system, the endocrine system continues to produce these effects for a prolonged period of time, often weeks or months. The sympathetic nervous system is like a match – easy to light and goes out fast – but the endocrine response is more like a fire – slow to get going but it lasts longer.

Cortisol is a vital hormone for protecting us from harm. It is key in enhancing those body functions that need to be working well to help protect us; as we have seen, it diverts extra oxygen to the muscles so we can flee if necessary. It also slows down processes that are not vital for our immediate survival; digestion, for example. Cortisol helps to alert us to danger and is a very important part of the danger-alert system but if cortisol levels remain elevated for prolonged periods of time, it can be a hindrance rather than a help. Some of the problems associated with raised cortisol levels include poor sleep, fatigue, depression and *poorer* physical performance.

Danger-alert hormones can exacerbate back pain, but other hormones can help to ease it. Oxytocin, which is produced in the pituitary gland, affects the body in many ways, from speeding up childbirth, relieving pain, preventing weight gain and making us feel good. Oxytocin is an easy chemical for us to manufacture – just hugging someone, or watching something pleasurable can cause the release of oxytocin.

## The immune system

The immune system, like the endocrine system, is powerful and is designed to look after you, especially when things go wrong. Scientific research has increased our knowledge of this immensely complex system in recent years and we now know that the immune system is a key player in pain states. The immune system has very close links with the adrenaline - and cortisol-based systems and, of course, the brain. Your immune system knows you, has memories of previous events (think of vaccinations and allergies), and will react when you are suffering from injury, illness or psychological distress.

Long-term stress and pain usually lead to an alteration in the activity of the immune system, which results in changes in the circulation of a type of cells known as cytokines, which are involved in signalling. These cytokine changes can *increase* the sensitivity of the nervous system and tissues and make you feel worse. The immune system, like other systems, can be activated not just by events that are actually occurring in the tissues but by the brain's interpretation of events. Consequently, if you *think* something is really bad, those thoughts and feelings can lead to an immune response.

The good news is that you can counteract these processes that combine to cause pain and boost the immune system to aid healing. All the strategies we suggest in this book to help 'turn down' pain are also known to help improve the function of the immune system. We really are treating the whole mind-body system with this approach.

To summarise, the autonomic nervous system, endocrine and immune systems will respond when our danger-alert system is activated. Remember: in acute pain these are normal responses to protect us from danger and are helpful to ensure our survival. The problem comes, however, when these systems remained locked-on. This can be a key contributor to persisting pain and poor function in people with back pain.

The final part of helping you to understand back pain relates to what happens in the nervous system at a biological level when the danger-alert system remains 'locked-on'. This helps you to understand why back pain and back-related disability can become persistent.

## Changes in the nervous system when pain persists

The nervous system is an amazing and adaptable system that is able to change its structure, depending on what it is exposed to. It will respond to most demands that it is faced with. Like a muscle that is used frequently, it gets stronger the more demands are made on it. New neural circuits are created within minutes of a demand, and if the demands continue, the circuits develop further. The late physiotherapist Louis Gifford put it succinctly in his book *Topical Issues in Pain*: 'Neurones that fire together wire together,' he said. But, conversely, if you stop using a circuit it gets weaker: 'Neurones that fire apart wire apart.'

So the more we do an activity, the stronger the neural circuits become. The less we do an activity, the weaker these circuits become. Nerve pathways can connect relatively distant areas of the nervous system together, and each time we think, feel or repeat an action, we strengthen this pathway. New thoughts and skills will carve out new pathways, and repetition and practice will strengthen these pathways. We all therefore have the ability to rewire our own central nervous systems.

Scientists have discovered that actual structural changes soon start to occur in many parts of the nervous system when neural circuits are repeatedly used. So, when those sensors from your back keep sending danger messages to your spinal cord, or when the neural pathways coming down from the brain turn up the danger-alert cells in the spinal cord, the nervous system starts to rewire itself. Very quickly, often within a few minutes, it becomes more efficient at sending danger messages up to the brain, by carving out new pathways. It does this by growing more neurones to alert us to danger.

The result of this is that your pain experience becomes stronger and your back starts to hurt even more. Sensations that previously felt fine, such as someone lightly touching the area, start to become painful as the rewiring takes hold and the painful area becomes increasingly sensitive. As long as the brain continues to compute that there is a threat, it produces danger-alert signals to keep the danger messages going, even when the tissues of the back have healed. If the brain keeps computing danger, it lays down more and more danger pathways, which are continually strengthened. When this happens, the pain becomes persistent.

*The good news is that we now know these changes can be reversed and we will show you how to do it in later chapters.*

As well as changes in the spinal cord, we know that structural changes also occur in the brain. Our brains start to make more chemicals and new circuits capable of winding up the pain. If you hurt your back while lifting a heavy box at work, for example, every time you see a heavy box, or watch someone else lifting a heavy box, it will switch on that danger circuit in your brain to remind you that lifting boxes might be threatening. Your brain prepares new networks to protect you from future problems. Of course, lifting a heavy box might not be painful next time, but your brain provides you with a best guess of what might happen, and produces a pain output. These new circuits become more established, with stronger pathways that are maintained as long as our brain concludes there is a threat. This all happens at a sub-conscious level, without us even being aware of it. The nervous system is gradually becoming more sensitised and the pain seems to take on a life of its own. We've listed some of the key features of a sensitised nervous system in the box on page 52.

It is possible to reset a sensitised system, first by helping people to understand what has happened biologically, and secondly by testing whether the activity they perceive as a danger is genuinely dangerous. This forms part of the pathway to recovery. If someone fears lifting boxes, for example, we might suggest they try to lift a small, light box; they will find it is not as bad as they thought, will feel less threatened by that particular activity and will then activate the pathways that can turn down the danger-alert volume. Once those pathways have been activated, it is likely that they will be able to lift more boxes, strengthening that pathway and gradually taking away the fear of lifting. This can help them to feel more confident about other activities that made them fearful. Once they try them, they might find they aren't so bad after all.

Understanding how to break patterns and habits that are harmful to our nervous system, and develop new patterns and habits that are healthy for our nervous system, can promote recovery. This is certainly the case with persistent back pain problems. In chapter 8 we will look at how to move freely and comfortably, and chapter 6 looks at ways of managing daily activity.

We also know that ongoing negative thoughts about our back pain can result in changes within our biology. All thoughts and feelings we experience are the result of chemicals released in the brain and nerve impulses between different neurones. Thoughts like 'Even the MRI scan hasn't been able to find what is damaged', or 'That doctor doesn't believe I have pain', or 'I'll never get back to how I was before', or 'My life is ruined by pain', or 'I shall never run again', are very threatening to a brain concerned about your survival. These thoughts are driven by fear, anger and/or depression and really do increase and maintain pain states. They act like a virus on a computer, corrupting messages and distracting from what needs to be done. They are very common in people with persistent pain. They are often enough to take you right to the edge of despair and hopelessness.

## The sensitised alarm system – some key features

- The back pain has gone on longer than three or four months.
- As we grow more neurones that alert us to danger in the area of the body that hurts, the pain starts to spread to other areas, sometimes nearby and sometimes a distance away from the original area. It's as if the back pain has taken on a life of its own.
- We would normally expect back pain to improve over time, but often with a sensitised system it gets worse.
- Small amounts of activity often result in large amounts of back pain. Activities you could previously do comfortably, such as enjoying a long walk or washing your car, become painful quite quickly for no apparent reason. The danger-alert system is still trying to protect you long after any damaged tissues have healed.

- Your back pain varies hugely from day to day: some days aren't too bad, but on other days the pain is intense and horrible.
- Sometimes you get sharp stabs of pain without even moving.
- You might get pain a long time after you have finished an activity; it may not have hurt whilst you were doing the shopping, but it hurt considerably when you got home.
- You notice your back pain is worse when you feel depressed or upset or angry. It may feel worse when you are anxious about something. Conversely you may notice your back pain is better on days when you are busy and distracted.
- You notice your back pain is worse in the presence of certain people or in certain situations. It could be that some people make you feel threatened and this feeds into your back pain. Or perhaps a location where you experienced distress or trauma in the past brings on a reaction in the present. The brain will subconsciously detect this and can produce a pain response.
- Treatments that used to help in the past no longer work, and sometimes make your pain feel worse. This could be physical treatments like massage, acupuncture or manual therapy, or it could also be analgesics.
- You find yourself withdrawing from certain activities, as you predict they will hurt. You stop accepting invitations to social events, turn down offers of work, or avoid playing sport with friends as you are convinced that you will feel worse afterwards.

We see many signs of sensitisation in people with persistent back pain. You may not have all the features listed in the box above. You can have persistent back pain which impacts on your life without your back feeling sensitive to touch, for example. But however your pain presents, simple tasks like bending down to tie a shoelace become very painful; getting up from the floor sometimes becomes impossible without significant pain; and carrying weights is highly likely to provoke pain.

The good news is that, in the same way as your nervous system grows new networks and connections to wind up the pain experience, we all have the ability to change this for the better. Once you are aware of the factors that might be contributing to your oversensitive nervous system, you can make changes that will retrain your nervous system and improve your health-related quality of life. Those connections that wind up the nervous system can be weakened by using a number of strategies we will discuss in the next few chapters, including setting meaningful goals, learning how to move with freedom and confidence, learning how to manage everyday activity levels, learning active relaxation strategies, and learning what triggers might be causing bad days or flare-ups. These strategies will combine to enhance the effectiveness of nature's inherent analgesic pathway, and your own pathway to recovery in your nervous system, thus improving your function and reducing your suffering. Think of it as turning up the control dial for comfort and turning down the control dial for pain and discomfort. Your confidence when using your back for everyday activities will improve.

Although all the changes associated with having an oversensitive nervous system sound alarming, they need not be. The brain is constantly adapting and changing every minute of the day. When pain becomes persistent these changes can be unhelpful and make the system more sensitive, but we know from recent developments that these changes can be reversed with training. Although back pain may seem to have taken over your life, your brain, with its billions of neurones and trillions of ever-changing connections has vastly greater capacities and abilities than just making pain.

To summarise, the nervous system will change its structure when back pain becomes persistent and, unless anything changes, the pain will persist. However, the good news is that this system is adaptable; persistent pain is not necessarily permanent and previous function can be restored. New research has helped us to understand that the nervous system *can* be retrained.

## The musculoskeletal system

With all of this talk about the nervous system, let's not forget what happens in the musculoskeletal system when back pain persists. It is widely accepted that persistent back pain has a direct impact on how we function. It is inevitable that as pain prevents us from carrying out many of the normal activities of daily life, deconditioning starts to set in. The normal, coordinated, free movement that we were previously capable of before the onset of back pain becomes hijacked, and as we continue to protect the painful area, the back slowly starts to stiffen up and decondition.

From a biological perspective the muscles of the back will actually start to waste, or atrophy, if pain persists for a prolonged period of time. This makes sustained activities difficult, as the muscles are unable to work for prolonged periods due to the effects of deconditioning. As well as becoming weaker, the muscle fibres will also shorten in length. You may notice this when you try to stretch your back in different directions. People tell us they can't stretch as far as they used to, and part of the reason for this is because the muscles have contracted or shortened.

The body continually adapts to the stresses and strains we put it through. If we protect it and avoid movement in response to back pain, the body adapts by shortening the muscles. Equally, if we don't use the full flexibility in our backs, we lose it. If the muscles become weaker and shorter, the joints in our back start to become stiffer. The ligaments and tendons around the joints also then start to shorten, which further impacts on our flexibility. As long as we continue (automatically, via the subconscious system, or by conscious choice) to protect ourselves from pain, these changes persist and will progress and become worse over time. In severe cases, people may find that simple activities such as moving from sitting to standing, bending to retrieve an item from a low cupboard, getting in and out of bed, getting on and off the floor, become extremely difficult. Walking can become challenging, so going to do the shopping becomes a huge effort and people have to resort to aids and adaptations such as walking sticks, or wheelchairs in the most severe cases.

The good news is that these changes are reversible: muscles can be built up again, ligaments and tendons can be stretched regularly to allow more flexibility and movement, and you will be guided how to do this in the following chapters.

Many of the changes in the musculoskeletal system of those suffering from persistent back pain are due to the effects of deconditioning, but it doesn't stop there. As you become less active, you may start to put on weight. Being overweight is an often overlooked complication of deconditioning and immobility. Excess weight may further overload a deconditioned back, adding to the cycle of persistent pain, and it will impact on other areas of the body, particularly knees and hips.

Sometimes when the back is less flexible, people start to rely on their knees to bend down towards the floor. But, as the knees have become deconditioned because there is less activity and the muscles start to atrophy, the knee joints may struggle with the extra load they are being subjected to. Pain might also develop in the knees, hips and other parts of the body. Being overweight increases the risk of osteoarthritis developing in your joints and will increase the risk of a range of health conditions, including heart disease, high blood pressure, stroke, diabetes, high cholesterol, some cancers and reproductive problems. So it is advisable to find ways to stop yourself gaining excess weight by staying as active as possible, to prevent yet another vicious cycle setting in.

Once what started as mild but persistent back pain leads to deconditioning of the musculoskeletal system you could be at risk of other much more significant health complaints. Retaining an awareness of what might be happening in your musculoskeletal system when back pain persists is vital. Chapter 8 explains how to move with freedom and confidence in order to help you unlock your pathway to recovery and start to reverse some of the effects of deconditioning on your body.

These opening chapters have outlined some of the reasons – biological, psychological and social – why back pain persists and how it can have such a major impact on our function and quality of life. Now you have an understanding of what is happening when back pain persists, we can look at what you can do about it. This starts with planning your pathway to recovery. To do this, you first need to set some meaningful goals.

# CHAPTER 5

# SETTING GOALS TO HELP YOUR RECOVERY

When you set off on a journey, say to a holiday destination, you need to know where you are heading, some staging posts along the journey and how long it is going to take. You also need to consider things that might not go exactly to plan, factors that are outside of your control, and figure out how to deal with them. Logical. And it's exactly the same for your recovery from persistent back pain. To help discover your pathway to recovery you need to start by setting your compass in the direction in which you intend to travel. We call this goal setting.

During our time in clinical practice we have seen many people achieve meaningful goals, which had a remarkable effect on improving their health-related quality of life. Sometimes these were simple, short-term goals, such as being able to walk to their local shop; others were more challenging, such as hiking to the top of their favourite mountain or completing a long-distance bike ride. Not surprisingly, managing these achievements has a powerful positive effect on self-esteem, confidence and self-belief. Even if they are still experiencing some discomfort, those pursuing goals are able to realise that pain need not be a life-restricting problem for them. They often tell us they feel as if they are back to their normal selves, and friends and relatives notice all sorts of positive changes. This is very encouraging, and helps them to maintain motivation to set further goals for recovery while hanging onto the progress already made. This can be a life-changing process for people who have struggled for years on end with the impact of back pain on their quality of life. Setting meaningful goals is the first essential part of your recovery plan.

Reflect for a moment on the pain biology you have learned so far. You can now appreciate how setting goals and starting to think about, visualise and plan for recovery will help to activate the brain's natural analgesic pathway. Even just *thinking* about a goal, and visualising yourself doing it, will activate this pathway and make you feel more confident that you can achieve it. We will look at ways of using visualisation to help you achieve your desired goals in chapter 9.

## Goal setting

Goal setting can be difficult at first, because when back pain persists it is sometimes hard to remember what life was like before. We can easily forget what it felt like to enjoy the pleasure of doing something physically active, such as a country walk, or enjoying an evening out with friends, or the satisfaction of craftwork and hobbies.

When in pain, it is common for people to lapse into what are known as 'black-or-white' thinking patterns: 'Either I am in pain and it's awful, or I am not in pain and life is wonderful.' In fact, no aspect of life is like this and pain most certainly isn't. This pattern of thinking is associated with high levels of emotional arousal and generates a huge amount of extra stress, thus fuelling the furnace of pain. Everything we experience sits along a spectrum in shades of grey rather than at the extremes of black and white.

Before starting to set goals, make sure you feel ready. It is part of being human to find reasons to resist making changes and maintain the status quo. We all do this to some extent: it helps to keep a sense of equilibrium in our lives and avoids the discomfort and uncertainty that change can bring. Humans are very adaptable and many adapt to a life in which they come to believe that recovery from pain is unlikely. This pattern of thinking sets in and can be hard to shift. Excuses why they can't attempt something are out of their mouths before they have even thought it through. But if you are able to contemplate a better quality of life and better function, however small the changes might be, then goal setting will help you to prepare for recovery.

It is normal to waver between committing to change and staying just as you are. This is known as ambivalence. We can remain in an ambivalent state about something that needs changing for a very short time or a very long time. Ambivalence, by the way, generates a lot of stress in the mind-body system. If you need a push to get you started, think of the example of someone who has toothache but has been putting off ringing the dentist to make an appointment. The moment they make that call, they start to feel better. That's what it will be like when you start to set goals.

Identifying and setting some goals that are meaningful to you shows that you are ready to take action. You can then apply yourself to making the changes. And once you have achieved your goals you can switch to maintaining the changes you have made and perhaps choose some further goals.

Remember that you are embarking on a journey. You have set your compass in the direction you want to travel and have some idea where you are heading. Now consider what the captain of an aeroplane or ship does before departure. They check they have everything they might need before starting off. They check the load they are carrying. Are there any unnecessary loads on board that might cause problems? They try to plan for the unexpected. They check the weather forecast to see if any storms are imminent that might best be avoided.

Have you the time and space in your life at present to give the journey your attention and commitment? Are your loved ones prepared to support and encourage you? If returning to work is your goal and you are in an employed situation, is your manager prepared to support a phased return, if that is deemed helpful? If you are self-employed, are you able to pick up work at a pace that suits your recovery or are you at risk of being swamped by work you feel unable to turn away? Is there some aspect of your life that is outside your control at present, something that may need more time to resolve? Think this through carefully. If you are in doubt, you might be better advised to put this book down for a while or seek advice about factors you are unsure about. Not making adequate preparations for the journey before starting is the most common reason for stalling.

## Dealing with ambivalence

If you want to change but are struggling to find the motivation then you are most likely in a stage of ambivalence. Ambivalence is the internal argument we have with ourselves when it comes to making decisions. It is a question of balance: on the one side are all the reasons why we would be best to stay as we are, and on the other side are the benefits that will come our way if we make changes. Remember that the status quo, our current situation, is familiar and can easily become a natural default position because change brings with it uncertainties.

To help you understand your own ambivalence, make a list of all the reasons why you might want to stay as you are and then a list of all the reasons to change your current situation. The box below may give you some pointers.

| Reasons to change | Reasons to stay as you are |
| --- | --- |
| I want to get off these tablets | It seems too much effort and might make the pain worse |
| I'd love to be able to go on holiday again; I miss travelling | I wouldn't be able to cope with the journey and sleeping in a different bed |

| I'd love to go for a long walk in the countryside, to breathe fresh air and look at the natural world | What if I was miles from anywhere and couldn't walk any further? It's better not to try, just in case |
|---|---|
| I'd love my children/partner/family/friends to see me return to fitness | I don't want to try and then fail. That would make everything worse than it already is |

Now make your own list and see what you come up with, weighing up the reasons for and against changing your current situation to a new and better one. Do the reasons to stay as you are sound like excuses?

If you are still struggling to find reasons why change is a good idea, consider the ways in which your back pain is influencing your life. Sometimes we don't realise, because they sneak up on us and it is almost subconscious when you refuse invitations and cut back on hobbies. Have a look at the following list and decide if any of them apply to you:

- I'm unable to socialise with friends the way I used to
- I can't play ball games with my children
- I can't do the garden any more
- I depend on others for help and feel guilty about it
- I don't like taking so much medication
- I'm gaining weight because I can't exercise
- I feel depressed and can't see a brighter future
- I can't work and have no income
- I can't keep up with the housework
- I move so awkwardly that I look older than my years
- I can't drive any more
- I'm losing friends because I am seldom able to see them

If you recognise yourself in several of these statements, using a goal-setting approach will help you to overcome them, one by one. As you approach the stage when you are ready to set a goal, have an inner argument with yourself – and maybe discuss it with your loved ones – to decide which goals are most important.

Another method that works well for some is to imagine that you have a twin alongside you. This twin knows you through and through, knows what is best for you, and is prepared to speak honestly and say what needs to be said. What is your twin saying to you? Listen carefully and be honest.

## What's your coping style?

Another thing to consider before setting a goal is your personal coping style. Every day we face many challenging situations we need to cope with. Coping is the ability to identify, manage and overcome the issues that stress us. There are many different ways to cope and coping skills vary enormously from person to person. Don't worry if you are not particularly good at coping because the skills can be learnt.

When it comes to pain, the most effective coping skills include problem solving, seeking knowledge and understanding, and then changing thoughts, behaviours and beliefs. Coping with your pain means you have the power to change it. Coping aims to change the threat value of different cues, which will in turn change the thoughts and feelings that those cues trigger, and the associated biological effects too – in essence, turning down the danger-alert system.

Most coping strategies can be categorised as either active or passive. A large body of research demonstrates that active strategies are more effective than passive strategies when it comes to helping people with persistent pain, and a variety of other health issues too. There are some examples in the box below.

| Active coping strategies | Passive coping strategies |
| --- | --- |
| Seeking better understanding of a problem | Avoiding any activities you associate with pain |
| Exploring different ways to move and do things | Putting your feet up and resting |

| | |
|---|---|
| Accepting the pain and planning ways to limit the impact it has on your daily life | Swallowing analgesic tablets |
| Staying positive and keeping an open mind | Waiting for external circumstances to change |
| Taking back control of flare-ups and setbacks | Waiting for someone else to make changes for you |
| Making plans, setting small, attainable goals and moving gradually towards them | |
| Setting longer-term goals and being patient as you set about achieving them | |

The guidance in this book is based on applying *active* coping strategies to unlock your pathway to recovery. If you identify more with the passive coping strategy list, then you may have to change your way of thinking to gain better personal control of your back pain.

If, having considered all these factors, you feel you are now ready to commit to an action plan that will take you on a pathway to recovery, it is time to set some goals that will help to restore your mobility and your quality of life.

## Choose goals that are meaningful to you

One of the most important parts of goal setting is to identify goals that are meaningful to *you*, and that will help in some way to meet your essential life needs. Those around you may have their own goals for you, but it is essential that you iden-tify goals of your own, based on things that are important to you. They should be things that will make your life better, and will have a positive influence on your comfort and mobility while reducing your pain. Goals made to satisfy other people are unlikely to help you so much.

We often encourage people to think of things they used to do in the past that made them 'tick'. It could be a favourite hobby or pastime that gave them a lot of satisfaction. Returning to previously enjoyed activities, initially at low levels, will deliver a great boost to self-confidence and help you to feel you are starting to restore function.

Sometimes goals are focused around medical issues. Many of the people we have helped have chosen to reduce their reliance on medication and have set this as one of their goals, with very favourable outcomes.

By setting goals that are meaningful to you, you are activating nature's inherent analgesic pathway. We know from studying the biology of persistent pain that this pathway to recovery will release powerful neurotransmitter chemicals that will help to turn down the volume dial on your pain and allow you to start feeling better.

### Pete's return to the tennis court

Pete had been struggling with back pain for over two years since a sudden episode at work one day. Although he had managed to continue working in a sedentary, office-based job, he had felt unable to play tennis for many months, and was relying on medication to get him through the day. Tennis was Pete's main recreational interest; it was what motivated him to take exercise; he had friends at the tennis club that provided his main social contact outside work. His wife often remarked how grumpy he had become since he stopped playing. She knew how important tennis was to her husband.

Pete also took pride in keeping his garden looking good. After several months of neglect because of his back pain, it had become untidy and overgrown, so this too was adding to Pete's sense of frustration. But he was focused on abolishing his pain completely before returning to tennis and gardening. He identified abolition of pain as his only goal. He firmly believed he needed to get rid of all his pain, and that recovery could only start once he was pain-free. A reasonable belief many might say – but it was holding up his recovery.

We asked Pete to consider a different approach. Instead of focusing on curing his pain first, we encouraged him to set goals around increasing his function. After thinking about this, Pete chose as his initial goal to get himself fit enough to play tennis again. He realised this was too much to start with so he broke that bigger goal down into several smaller goals. After we had helped him to understand that it would not do any harm if he started off gently, Pete decided to practise his tennis service in the back garden, hitting a ball against his garden wall. Initially he would use half of his normal serve, and try it for just ten minutes. This was his first goal. After doing this twice a day for a week he felt confident enough to progress to his next goal, which was visiting the tennis club on his own. He chose to do this on his own because he identified a potential pitfall here: he has a very competitive streak and if he started alongside his fitter friends at the club, he knew he would not be able to stop himself overdoing it, which might risk him sliding all the way down the recovery ladder. Using a small basket of balls, Pete started to enjoy playing on his own against the tennis wall; the feeling of hitting the ball in an environment that was familiar to him gave him much pleasure. He focused his mind on driving the ball a fraction of the power he would have done when fully fit. To release tension from his body during the strokes he applied a technique that we had coached him in: he released his breath fully as he drove through the ball, rather than bracing himself by holding his breath. It is a remarkably common habit in people with back pain to hold their breath in an attempt to protect themselves.

All of this was a natural distraction from Pete's habit of dwelling on how his back was feeling. He congratulated himself for the achievements he had made. Soon he felt confident enough to book a court with a friend to play one set of tennis. He asked his friend to be patient with him at this stage, and to keep the competitive sparring for another day. After their game, Pete noticed that his back was feeling more comfortable. He did not need to take any analgesic tablets. His sleep pattern was improving too.

Next he applied the same approach to the gardening, setting an initial goal of gardening for ten minutes then doing a little bit more each time. This was challenging because he acknowledged he was (like many people) of a 'get the job finished by a certain time even if it exhausts me' mindset. He had to accept that he might not finish weeding a flower bed or mowing the lawn one particular day but could return to it at a later date.

Some months afterwards, we saw Pete again and he told us he was feeling good. His wife came along with him and she said she was much happier too. Pete was playing recreational tennis with his friends, his garden was back the way he liked it and his mood had improved enormously. His back still ached from time to time but he no longer allowed it to dominate his life. Setting goals focusing around restoring function rather than curing pain were helpful for him, and they will be for you too in the longer term.

## How to structure your goals

One of the best ways to achieve goals is to structure your goal in a way that allows you to measure progress over a period of time. In our experience we have found the 'SMART' formula particularly helpful. SMART is an acronym for Specific, Measurable, Achievable, Rewarding and Time-Orientated. This approach allows you to name some clear and tangible goals that you can work towards, and it can be helpful to look at your goals in this context.

## Specific

Firstly, make your goal specific. A goal such as 'I want to feel better' is too abstract, because 'feeling better' is difficult to quantify. It is much more helpful to select something tangible, such as 'I want to return to recreational walking' or 'I want to be able to go swimming at the local pool'. So think about a particular activity you want to be able to do – or a new skill you want to learn – but keep it specific. Visualising yourself achieving the goal can be helpful (see page 146 for more on visualisation).

## Measurable

Next, use a form of measurement to identify the goal. A goal such as 'I want to walk up a hill' is too vague, as hills can vary in size, shape, length and terrain. It is helpful to set a more tangible goal, such as 'I want to complete a 2 km walk up and down my favourite hill'. This makes it clearer so you will be able to measure when you have managed to reach the goal.

## Achievable

Make sure you have enough time available to spend on what-ever task you set for yourself. There will inevitably be other demands on your attention. You will need to give and take. Allotting more time for one task means you have less time for others. What can you drop? It is remarkably common for people to heap one more task onto the 'to-do' list believing that somehow they will make time for it. You cannot 'make' time, and it can be disheartening if you feel you aren't achieving your goals, when it is simply because there aren't enough hours in the day. So make sure you allocate enough time to achieve your goals on the path to easing your persistent back pain.

Try to think of any practical implications. For example, if you want to be able to swim 30 lengths but your nearest swimming pool is 20 miles' drive away and you can only access the pool at certain hours, you may not be able to get there regularly enough. On top of that the pressure of the extra travelling might build up more stress, rather than alleviating it. It is helpful to work out whether the goal you set can be practically achieved. If you choose something unachievable, you will feel defeated. Remember that these negative thoughts and feelings are brain impulses that will activate the fight-flight-freeze response and serve to amplify and perpetuate pain. You have a choice. Make sure your goal is within reach and achievable.

## Rewarding

Having a goal that will make you feel good to achieve is very rewarding. Obvious. As we have mentioned earlier, people around us may have other goals for us, which meet their needs more than ours, but they would not make us feel so rewarded. Think about what will improve your own quality of life. If you previously enjoyed the buzz you got from playing music in a band, this would be a suitable goal for you. If you enjoy painting watercolours, go ahead. In chapter 12 we will look at the importance of getting essential life needs (not wants) met. Aim to work on goals that will help you get these needs met in a balanced way.

## Time-Orientated

Setting a clear time frame in which to achieve your goal helps to get you motivated. If there is no time frame progress can slip as you put things off for days or weeks. You are then in danger of slipping back into an ambivalence phase as the brain starts up that inner dialogue, finding reasons to justify why you are not making progress, or deciding that it might be better not to bother at all. Here are some examples of time-orientated goals:

- I want to be fit enough to return to my Zumba dance class in six weeks' time.
- I want to be able to walk a kilometre to my local shop and return again carrying a light rucksack in four weeks' time.
- I want to taper off the analgesic medication and finish with it completely four weeks from now.

Setting goals using this approach will allow you to have a clear focus on your target and how you are going to reach it.

## Joe Simpson's sunbeam

Joe Simpson is a mountaineer who, during a descent of Siula Grande, a mountain in the Peruvian Alps, fell and broke his right leg. He ended up stuck at the bottom of a 100-metre crevasse, alone, without assistance and with little hope of survival as he was unable to weight-bear through his right leg. He was in a hopeless situation, but this didn't stop him believing he could survive, if he could only formulate a plan and see a target ahead of him. The following passage is from his book, *Touching the Void*.

'A pillar of gold light beamed diagonally from a small hole in the roof, spraying bright reflections off the far wall of the crevasse. I was mesmerised by this beam of sunlight burning through the vaulted ceiling from the real world outside. It had me so fixated that I forgot about the uncertain floor below and let myself slide down the rest of the rope. I was going to reach that sunbeam. I knew it then with absolute certainty. How I would do it, and when I would reach it were not considered. I just knew.

'In seconds, my whole outlook had changed. The weary frightened hours of night were forgotten, and the abseil which had filled me with such claustrophobic dread had been swept away. The twelve despairing hours I had spent in the unnatural hush of this awesome place seemed suddenly to have been nothing like the nightmare I had imagined. I could do something positive. I could crawl and climb and keep on doing so until I had escaped from this grave. Before, there had been nothing for me to do except lie on the bridge trying not to feel scared and lonely, and that helplessness had been my worst enemy. Now I had a plan.'

## The difference between goals and dreams

A *goal* is entirely within your own ability to achieve. You hold all the control levers.

A *dream* or *aspiration* is something that you wish for. You have many control levers in your own hands to make it happen but crucially not all of them – someone else or other circumstances will influence your ability to achieve your dream.

It is important to understand the difference. For example, Donna's *dream* is to win the national championship 800-metre running race in July. Having achieved some good results during the season, she is in with a chance. However, so are at least six other athletes of similar ability. She cannot control everything that happens during the national championships, such as the weather conditions, the form and tactics of the other athletes, and any unforeseeable circumstances such as sudden illness or injury. Her *goal* is to do the very best physical and mental preparation that she can, such as training hard and eating an optimum diet, and that is within her ability to influence. By focusing on her goals she sets herself up for success: whatever happens, she did her best and can do no more.

However, if she chooses the dream as her goal then there is a better than evens chance that she will not succeed and she will then be at risk of perceiving herself to have failed in some way. More importantly from a psychological point of view, she might see herself as having been personally responsible for that failure. This creates internally driven stress. If you have a pain problem, failing to achieve a goal might cause the pain to flare up, as memories of other times you have 'failed' are brought to the front of your mind by a pattern match in the subconscious part of your brain. Top sports people train their minds as well as their bodies to prevent this happening.

However, you can use goals to achieve dreams, as the following examples show.

- *'I want to get back to work after being absent for three months due to back pain.'* This is the dream. It depends on the work still being available after three months away, and the willingness of the manager and the others who have been covering for you during your absence to be flexible. The goals you could set might include: 1) arrange a meeting with the manager to discuss your plans and ask about returning to your normal job, perhaps in a phased return; 2) work on any aspect of your physical fitness that will help you return to and maintain your job role; and 3) learn and practise a plan to manage flare-ups of back pain so as to reduce the risk of having to take time off sick again.
- *'I want to play doubles tennis again after 18 months out of the game due to back pain.'* This is the dream. It depends on others playing with you at a level you can manage until your full fitness returns. You may have to swallow some pride here if you are in a club. The goals could include: 1) work on aspects of your physical fitness (perhaps hitting the ball against a wall on your own to begin with) so that you can start to play again at a basic level within six weeks; 2) find a friend who is prepared to play knock-about, non-competitive tennis with you on a full-sized court to help build up your confidence as your fitness improves.

- *'I want to improve the quality of my sleep.'* This is the dream. It can be difficult to get a good night's sleep when your back hurts, but there are a number of things you can do. The first step is to change any aspects of your sleeping environment and night-time routine that might impair sleep quality (see the section on sleep hygiene on page 140 in chapter 9 to help you with this).

## Focus on the future

When the onset of back pain is associated with an accident, perhaps at work or on the road, it can lead to a sense of feeling a victim; someone else is to be blamed and must be made to pay for the suffering you have been put through. Such an incident will inevitably be associated with strong feelings. Anger, rage, helplessness and guilt are some of the common feelings people experience after trauma. These feelings are very likely to wind up pain through constant activation of the fight-flight-freeze system. The pain, and the loss of function associated with pain, are likely to persist and be resistant to attempts to alleviate them until there is either a change of attitude or closure on the incident. It can be very difficult for some people to let go of these feelings, for understandable reasons. For example, it can be very difficult to accept the injustice of being knocked down by a reckless car driver until either they have been punished or you have received compensation – or both. It can be very difficult to set goals in this situation. You do, however, have a choice: devoting your energy and attention to getting on with the rest of your life rather than dwelling on what has happened will help your recovery.

So take your time. If you are unsure about the approach we have discussed so far then it might be better to pause, put this book down and come back to it another time. It's OK to be unsure. Sometimes choices are difficult to make. We all go through ambivalent stages in different areas of life: for example, we might be uncertain about applying for a new job, moving house, getting married, getting divorced, giving up smoking, returning to work or losing weight. Sometimes circumstances need to change before we feel ready to take action and set goals for ourselves.

If you feel ready, let's look at how you can manage your daily activity levels, and design your own personal pathway to recovery.

# CHAPTER 6

# HOW TO MANAGE YOUR DAILY ACTIVITY

Many of the people with persistent back pain we see at the Royal Orthopaedic Hospital have had to adapt their activity levels. This has often had a huge impact on their quality of life, and makes it difficult for them to plan ahead. They find there are good and bad days, so social engagements are frequently rearranged, while leisure pursuits and work opportunities diminish as their ability to manage them declines. On some days they find they can manage a lot of activity, but they almost always pay for it later with a flare-up of pain which means they have to rest again. This is very frustrating and sets up an ongoing cycle of impaired function, which contributes to keeping the nervous system sensitive and maintaining back pain.

However, it doesn't have to be like this; there is a way to address it successfully. To do this you first need to look at how you currently manage your activity on a day-to-day basis.

## Have you learned to avoid activities that hurt?

If we have a bad experience, we are less likely to repeat that same activity in the future. Imagine going out for a meal to a restaurant where the starter was cold, the wine was warm, the service was slow and the waiters were rude. You leave early, as the manager isn't prepared to acknowledge your poor experience, and you feel annoyed. You warn your friends to avoid going there. You learn from your first visit that the restaurant is unpleasant and this motivates you to avoid going back there.

The same learning process occurs when back pain becomes persistent. Because the sensation is unpleasant, the logical thing to do is to avoid it. The best way to do this is to learn to avoid activities that feel unpleasant. You just don't go there. However, in time this strategy is a slippery downwards slope. It becomes a habit and leads to you withdrawing from more and more activities. This may have relatively minor consequences, or might lead to major consequences as a whole way of life comes to a grinding halt.

What makes matters worse is that the brain confuses *association* with *causation*. A classic error and a leap of faith. Simply because pain is *associated* with a particular activity does not mean that activity is the *cause* of the pain.

Avoidance of activity is a learned response, but the good news is that it can unlearned, allowing you to recover function and improve your quality of life. We will look at how to do this later in this chapter.

## Avoidance and damage beliefs

Some (but not all) people with persistent low back pain learn to avoid activity because they fear they are going to cause more damage to their back and they develop worrying thoughts associated with this fear. But fear can play a key role in preventing recovery from back pain. In chapter 3, we explained that ongoing pain is not a reliable indicator of whether there is damage in the back. However, if you are fearful that damage is being caused, it may seem as if the logical thing to do is avoid activities you associate with pain, which you have come to believe are the cause of the problem, as figure 10 illustrates.

Figure 10 - Fear about damage can prevent recovery.

If you tend to avoid activities because you are worried they will cause damage to your back, it is helpful to understand that this is highly unlikely. In almost all cases of persistent back pain, increasing activity is achievable and positively good for you.

Remember: if you have a tendency to avoid some activities in response to your back pain, physical changes start to develop in your body. The all-important muscles and ligaments in your spine will start to become deconditioned and physical changes start to occur in the nervous system too.

## Pain, the brain and our body map

Every part of our body is mapped in the hemispheres of our brain. This map is ordered in a very specific way, with the toes represented at the top of the hemispheres and the mouth at the bottom. The number of neural connections in our brain linked to any given body area is not decided by the size of the body area, but by how many complex neural connections are required for its functioning. The result of this is that small but very sensitive areas of the body, such as the tongue, lips, or thumbs, have a large mapped area in the brain, whilst some more extensive areas, such as our backs or legs, have a much smaller mapped area, as figure 11 shows. As a result of this, the brain map for all our body parts is distorted, and not representative of the size of the individual body part.

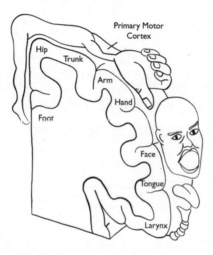

Figure 11 - The body mapped in the brain; scientists call this illustration the 'motor homunculus'.

Some amazing facts have been emerging from research into brains over the past few decades. We now know that brain maps are not fixed throughout our lives, like a map of the world – they have a tremendous ability to adapt, dependent on what activities we do regularly in our day-to-day life. For example, concert pianists will have much larger areas in their brain maps for their fingers and hands, as playing the piano requires millions more complex neural connections within the brain to allow them to play. These complex connections will be very different to those of the rest of the population, as pianists have trained these nerve-muscle connections over a long period and the brain has adapted in response to this.

So, we know from scientific studies that the brain and nervous system adapt and make more and stronger connections in response to demand. This applies whether the demand comes from thousands of hours of practising sport, creating art, speaking a foreign language, filling out crosswords, making crafts, or any other skill. In another example, we have all watched in amazement as tennis players play seemingly impossible shots time after time, at the edge of their abilities. The reason they can do this is because they have trained their nerve-muscle connections through repetition and practice, and changes have occurred in the areas of their brain map linked to the body parts they use in competition. Constant practice keeps the neural circuits tuned up for best performance.

It's just the same if the demand is for the nervous system to remain in a constant hyper-vigilant state to threat, as in persistent pain. However, the change in brain mapping occurs in the opposite way when we learn to avoid activity in response to pain. Studies have shown that the map in the brain representing the back becomes distorted in people with persistent back pain. In other words, *actual physical changes* occur in the brain structures in people with persistent low back pain, which are not seen in people without low back pain. This fits in nicely with the old adage that if we don't use it we lose it. It also helps to explain why people with persistent back pain, who have learned to avoid activity, find everyday movements such as bending, lifting and twisting so difficult. The complex nerve connections from the brain to the muscles of the back become redundant, making these activities become more difficult to complete. If you suffer with persistent back pain, you can probably think of several everyday activities you find difficult.

However, as in the case of the concert pianist or the professional tennis player, the good news is that the brain and nervous system are adaptable and, with repetition and practice, can recover. So if there are activities that you want to get back to doing, things that currently feel beyond you, don't give up. The new discovery that the nervous system is adaptable has helped to transform the ways we approach helping people with back pain to restore function and quality of life. We trust this gives you renewed hope: you have the potential to unlock the doors on your pathway to recovery. We will explore how to start putting a recovery plan in place later on in this chapter.

## Do you overdo it, then pay later?

So far we have only considered people who tend to avoid activity (for a variety of seemingly logical reasons) due to their back pain. However, while some reduce their activity in response to pain, others respond differently. They have good days when they seem to function very well, and are able to engage in relatively high levels of activity, but they then pay the price afterwards. They find that by overdoing activity on a good day, they will suffer the following day. This pattern repeats itself. The problem is that until it is pointed out that this habit maintains pain, the individual is likely to have no insight into what they are doing. It's the way they have always tended to respond to difficulties – keep trying harder, doing the same thing over and over again, until the problem goes away.

There are often very logical reasons why people overdo activity. For example, there always seems so much to do, or jobs have to be finished completely before they can rest. Even though they may have family and friends around them who encourage them to take things a bit easier, they often struggle to accept advice, and get caught in a cycle of over - and under-activity. This can make it difficult to plan their lives with any consistency. Underlying reasons for this very common pattern of behaviour include strong feelings of perfectionism, inability to delegate tasks, a desire to please others all of the time, or overcompensation in response to a setback in life.

Somewhat paradoxically, pushing too hard on good days is where they are going wrong.

We see many people who are caught in a vicious cycle of over-activity. Commonly they find it very difficult to say 'no'. Something has to give sooner or later, and they reach a point when they feel overwhelmed and can do no more. They then have to stop many activities completely for a short period until they recover. This is deeply frustrating and they typically berate themselves as failures. Of course, as we know, this keeps the pain volume turned up nice and loud and the vicious cycle develops further, as figure 12 demonstrates.

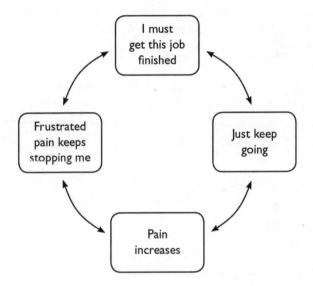

Figure 12 – The vicious cycle of overdoing activity

If you tend to overdo things then crash out with increased pain, you are generating massive amounts of stress that keep the nervous system hyper-vigilant and keep on winding up your pain. You will prevent recovery occurring until you learn to change your response and become more patient with yourself.

In the same way that inactivity weakens the connections between the brain map and back muscles, over-activity makes the nervous system even more sensitive, as we strengthen the neural circuits that generate pain responses. It is akin to feeding our nervous system with more energy, fuelling the system further. As this vicious cycle continues, less can be done even on a good day, while the bad spells get longer and despair sets in as there seems to be no way out.

Let's look at a real life story:

## Claire and her overloading job

Claire worked as an administrator in a small business and had been experiencing back pain for several months. Her boss regularly asked her to stay behind to do overtime, and continually overloaded her with work that she never had enough time to complete. However, Claire had been in the job for less than a year and wanted to impress her employers with her commitment and diligence. Every day she spent long hours at her desk completing tasks, and never so much as took a break for lunch. Over time, she noticed her back pain was becoming more and more bothersome during daily activities, but she tried hard to ignore it and soldier on. But things got worse. Claire found herself needing to go straight to bed when she got home, as her back pain was so bad. At weekends she could do very little. She stopped socialising with friends, as she felt she needed to rest. All in all, Claire had developed a miserable existence, with her life dominated by her pain.

We asked Claire to discuss her workload informally with her boss. She thought he would take a dim view, and told us she had been afraid to raise it with him. To her surprise, her boss said he had not realised the effect that piling more and more work onto her had caused. Between them they formulated a plan to delegate some of the work to other people, so that she felt less overloaded. Claire started to leave work on time, and learned to be more assertive with her boss. In time her back pain became much less troublesome and she regained a good quality of life outside of work.

We frequently see this over/under-activity cycle in our clinical work, in many different situations, both at home and in the workplace. It feeds pain by continually stoking up the physiological stress response and making the individual feel they have lost control over something they know they need to control. If you can identify relationships either at home or at work in which you find it difficult to say 'no', if you frequently find yourself resenting obligations and wondering why on earth you ever agreed to them when you would much rather not, if you are feeling increasingly exhausted or in pain, take a step back and identify ways to protect yourself from the vicious cycle. Perhaps a friend or your partner will suggest that you need to take more time for yourself and learn to say 'no' more often. Do not leave it until you have a complete breakdown or it will take you much longer to recover.

When you carve out time for yourself, when you say 'no' without feeling guilty, when you ask for help when it's needed, you will start to feel more relaxed and comfortable, you will sleep better and you will be more productive. And those around you will appreciate the benefits too.

## How avoidance and over-activity can both prevent recovery

Both avoidance and overdoing it are unhelpful in the long term and will block your pathway to recovery. Figure 13 demonstrates the impact that avoiding or overdoing activity can have on your ability to function and illustrates that while this habit continues, it is highly unlikely that function will improve in the long term. It will either get worse or stay the same if you maintain the same approach to activity. You have a choice.

Try to identify whether you tend to avoid or overdo activity, referring to the features listed in the box below. There

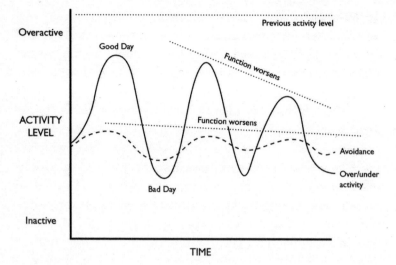

Figure 13 - How activity levels can influence pain and recovery.

will be some overlap and responses may vary according to the situation you are in. Write down whether you have a natural tendency to avoid certain activities, or to overdo activity. And be honest with yourself! Then think of the reasons that drive you to be this way, and write them down too.

| Avoids activity | Overdoes activity |
|---|---|
| I'm concerned I might damage myself | I can't say 'no' |
| I worry that pain means my back is being harmed | I would rather get the job finished 'even if it kills me' |
| I tried to do more but it hurt too much | No pain, no gain mentality |
| I've lost confidence in my back | No one can do the job as well as me, therefore it's pointless to ask others for help |
| I think my back needs fixing before activity levels can increase | It's better to have some good days even if I have to pay for it later with bad days |

# A graded approach to managing your activity levels

Whether you are stuck in a cycle of avoidance or over/under-activity, changing those habits is necessary to liberate yourself from the effects that persistent pain has on your daily life. Now it's time to discover how to apply a graded approach to activity.

It might feel wrong at first: if you have tended to avoid activity, any increase will be likely to increase discomfort in the short term; if you have tended to overdo activity then putting the brakes on will feel uncomfortable for you. This is normal but it is important to continue with your plan, even when you feel worse initially, in order to restore function and quality of life.

It is also OK to feel somewhat sceptical to start with. Habitual patterns of activity can be very hard to change. Just give it a try. Remember the marginal gains approach and know that even small beginnings are reconnecting neural circuits within your central nervous system. The more they get used, the stronger the connections become. Here's how to make a start.

- Choose an activity you wish to do more of; this could include walking, gardening, swimming, or travelling somewhere you like which is a reasonable distance away.
- Work out how much of that activity you can comfortably do now, without feeling you are overdoing it. You can measure this in time, distance, or any unit of measurement you like. If walking for 20 minutes makes you feel really uncomfortable when you get home, that's too much. If walking for 10 minutes feels OK, then start with 10 minutes. But go easy on yourself to begin with and don't push yourself too hard.
- Plan when you are going to do your chosen activity. Decide how many days in the week you will do it, and write down how much you will do. It is important to stick with the plan on both good and bad days.

- Carry out the plan over a period of one week. Expect to feel worse to begin with, particularly if you are increasing activity. This doesn't indicate anything is wrong with your body. It is a normal response to increasing levels of activity and should not alarm you. Make sure you don't overdo it on the good days. Stick to the plan.
- Review the plan at the end of the week. If you have been too ambitious and are pushing things too much, too quickly, you may need to re-set your plan and make the following week a little easier. Conversely, perhaps your activity plan is not ambitious enough and you find it very easy to reach your activity target. If this happens, you can increase your activity levels the following week. Take stock at the end of each week and try to increase your levels bit by bit.

The graded activity principles can be applied to any of the goals you set in chapter 5. When used correctly, you should see gradual improvement over time, as figure 14 illustrates.

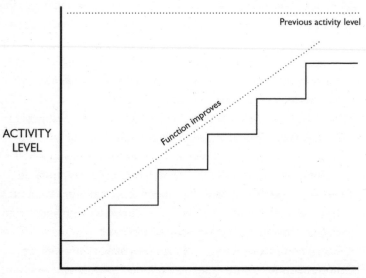

Figure 14 – Improving function through graded activity.

## Deborah learns graded walking

Deborah used to enjoy regular walks from her house into her local town. It provided her with social contact, gave her the opportunity to get some regular exercise and enhanced her sense of wellbeing. But for twelve months she had not been able to walk into town because of pain in her back. She found walking for short periods, usually 10 minutes, was quite enough for her, and after that she would have to sit down and rest. Her walk into town took 30 minutes, and was simply beyond her capabilities. This made her feel low and frustrated. Deborah's learned response to her pain was to avoid walking, because it felt really unpleasant.

With a new understanding of her pain, and using goal-setting methods, Deborah chose to do regular short walks of no more than 10 minutes' duration. She did this on days when she was feeling good and days when she was feeling not so good. For several days Deborah did a short 10-minute walk every day, irrespective of how she was feeling. Some days she managed it easily and it felt really pleasant, whilst on other days she just about managed it. However, she quickly learned that she could still do it, without any major unpleasant side-effects. She then started to do the 10-minute walk twice a day.

This progressed to 12 minutes for several days in succession, irrespective of how she was feeling. For the next few weeks, Deborah gradually increased the length of her walks to 14, 16, 18, 20 minutes, and so on. She sometimes felt a bit worse after an increase in the length of the walks but this did not last. To Deborah's surprise, she discovered that building her activity in a step-by-step manner wasn't too unpleasant after all.

Finally she built up the confidence to walk the 30 minutes into her local town, have a rest and then walk back again. It wasn't long before she was arranging to meet her friend in a coffee shop in town to catch up on much-missed conversation. Every time she did this, it reminded her that walking was pleasant, motivating her to continue with it. This new learning experience worked for her. She still had days when she wasn't feeling so good, but these were noticeably fewer in frequency and not so disabling for her. A graded approach allowed Deborah to return to an activity that gave her an enormous sense of wellbeing and achievement, which she was able to maintain in the long term.

Reflecting back, Deborah acknowledges that to begin with, increasing her activity level felt 'wrong'. It went against many of her preconceived ideas about back pain and activity. She had assumed that she would always feel worse if she increased her activity levels, and might even be causing actual damage to her back. But she didn't, and was able to turn things round for herself.

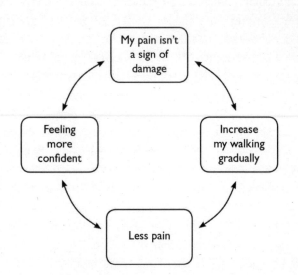

Figure 15 – Using graded activity to address fear of moving.

We now know that the brain and central nervous system are highly adaptable to the demands put on them. Scientists term this 'neural plasticity'. The amazing fact is that while you are still alive (and provided the brain is not structurally damaged by diseases such as Alzheimer's) the central nervous system will respond to what is called for and will lay down new connections in response to this – millions of them, even as we get older. Another way of viewing this is that our brains thrive on learning new ways of understanding, new skills, new patterns of movement, new stories, solving puzzles, untangling problems, and so forth. We learn by making new neural connections within the central nervous system.

The improvements in comfortable range of movement that we see within days of people starting to grade up their physical activity in a step-by-step way is primarily due to changes within the neural circuits in their central nervous system. Dormant neural pathways to muscle groups are being given a wake-up call and this releases tension in the muscles. It is not due to regaining 'strength' in the muscle groups; we know from scientific research that to strengthen muscles they need progressive loading over the course of several months. That will come later as physical activity progresses.

A graded activity approach allows the nervous system to start functioning more normally again. Whilst we may still have some ongoing pain, our tolerance to activity starts to improve, and the more evidence we gain that the approach is working, the more we are likely to continue with it.

Whilst Deborah's story illustrated how a graded approach can help someone who has become avoidant of activity, Andy's story (below) helps to illustrate how a graded approach can help those who adopt the over/under-activity cycle in response to their back pain.

## Andy's need to get the job done

Andy worked as a self-employed tree surgeon. He had built his company up over several years and prided himself on doing a good job and making sure his customers got value for money. His first episode of disabling back pain put him out of action for a couple of weeks but he managed to return to work with minimal disruption for his customers. However, over the next couple of years he kept experiencing recurrent episodes of back pain, each one lasting longer than the last. He found he never fully recovered from each episode but tried to keep working through his pain in order to keep his customers happy. On a good day he would work long hours, making the most of the reduction in symptoms, but then he had to put up with several bad days, when it was a real struggle to get through his work. This caused him to be very frustrated and he noticed he was losing business. He found it impossible to predict how well he would be able to function from day to day and that made it very difficult to be reliable for his customers.

With a new understanding of his pain, Andy chose to do something different. Graded activity didn't seem a logical suggestion, but he was prepared to give it a try. After all, he had nothing to lose, as previous methods were not working. He decided to limit the hours he worked on the good days, making sure he didn't push himself too hard. As he was driven to make sure he got the job done well, he found this difficult to begin with. He felt a strong urge to keep going and overdo it, but reminded himself of the likely consequences if he did.

He discovered that by modifying his activity levels on good days, he started to have fewer bad days and when they did occur they were not quite so bad as before. He began to record his back pain on a scale of 1 to 10 and this helped. Previously he had been in the habit of viewing days as either 'good' (10/10) or 'bad' (1/10) with no grades in between. The more he learned to modify his activity when he was feeling scores above 7/10, the more consistently comfortable he became and over the longer term he was more productive. He felt confident accepting work, knowing that he would be able to complete it. He also learned that he had been consistently underestimating the time each job took and this was giving his customers unrealistic expectations that he could not meet. As he was always keen to please his customers this put enormous additional and unnecessary stress on himself and wound up his pain. But his new graded approach meant he could judge exactly when a job would be finished and customers could rely on him to keep his word.

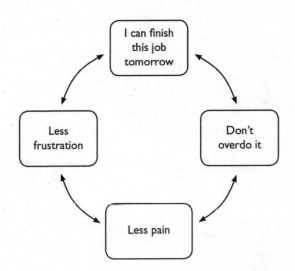

Figure 16 – Changing to use a graded approach.

## Keep setting more goals

One of the common pitfalls encountered when using a graded activity approach is that some people increase their activity a small amount but then stop. Although they have made progress, they stay within a safe 'bubble' of activity but don't push the boundaries further. Sometimes this is because they feel worse when they try to reach the next level of activity. Feeling worse at first can be a significant obstacle to progress. Try to ensure you keep working on a graded plan, and if you achieve your first short-term functional goal, then set another

SMART goal and work towards that. Combining goal setting with graded activity is the best way of helping you to restore function and quality of life.

We are sure you have been in a shopping mall or a railway station where there is an escalator and a staircase running parallel with each other and leading up to another level. The escalator is generally half the width of the staircase. You see a long line of people waiting to join the escalator yet no one seems to be using the stairs, even though there is ample room on them and they are going to the same destination. Pondering this, you notice that very few people waiting in the line are carrying anything you would consider heavy or bulky and they all look perfectly well and able-bodied.

It is a fact of human nature that given the choice of means to get to a destination, the default is to choose the easier option. Perhaps this derives from our evolutionary biology when, constantly on the move to find security, food or shelter, our chances of survival were greater if we took every opportunity to conserve energy. For many of us physical activity has systematically been removed from our lives and we are conditioned to labour-saving machines, the help of others, or the click of a computer mouse.

The way of unlocking your pathway to recovery from back pain and the disability it has caused you is to walk up the steps one at a time, keeping a focus all of the time on where you want to get to. Maybe take a brief pause in the middle to reflect on your journey so far.

The passive method of being conveyed upwards on an escalator does not work for those with persistent back pain. You need to take control into your own hands.

We have a couple more pieces of advice on the theme of stair-climbing. The journey will be much easier if you first off-load unnecessary baggage you have been carrying with you (for example, fear and avoidance beliefs about back pain, anger, grievances and other strong feelings that have outlived their usefulness). It also helps to walk up those steps

with others alongside you who understand the effort you are putting in. You have to take those steps yourself because you can't be pushed up – and if you were, you would fall down again very soon.

CHAPTER 7

# GETTING THE BEST OUT OF MEDICATION

For many people, medication has an important role when it comes to managing back pain. It can help you get through the difficult days, it can enable you to sleep better at night and can be a useful way to turn your pain volume down in the short term. However, medication for back pain also has many disadvantages and in some cases only makes matters worse.

In this chapter we will aim to help you understand what medication can and cannot do, identify the common pitfalls and learn what you can do about them, so that if you do use pills, you can get the best out of them, while minimising the side-effects. As with every other aspect of treatment, you have a choice when it comes to using medication and it pays to be as informed as possible.

Remember: this book can only be a guide, expressed in general terms. If you are in any doubt about the medicines you have been prescribed, we advise you to discuss the matter with your own doctor. All of the medications listed in this chapter, apart from paracetamol and some anti-inflammatory tablets, are prescription-only. If you have started taking either prescription drugs or over-the-counter medications and notice unwanted side-effects, you should consult your doctor. He or she will be able to review your medication, and suggest alternative options.

## Watch your language!

Let's stop and think for a moment about a word we commonly use in everyday language that can be misleading and set up unrealistic expectations. Medications prescribed for back pain are invariably referred to as 'painkillers'. We strongly advise you do not use this term. It is misleading. No medicine ever discovered so far can kill persistent pain. It is crucially important for those with persistent back pain to understand this.

It is much more helpful to use the term 'analgesic' because it better describes what pain medications are supposed to do – to relieve or ease pain. If the medicines you take, especially those described on the packet as 'strong', do not 'kill' your pain, then it is likely that the part of the brain that tries to protect you will conclude that the cause of your pain must be very serious indeed, or even incurable. This will inevitably set up more tension and wind up an already stressed danger-alert system. This is an example of a phenomenon called the nocebo effect. It means that predicting a poor outcome from a treatment can become a negative self-fulfilling prophecy – the exact opposite of the placebo effect.

Medicines prescribed by doctors can be roughly grouped into three categories:

- Medication to relieve or ease symptoms for a period of time, in order to help get you going again while nature takes its course. These might be used while you recover from injury or operation or during the period when you are waiting for an operation. People with persistent back pain are often prescribed these tablets, which may include anti-inflammatories, opioids and anti-depressants or anti-epileptic drugs, as well as injections of corticosteroids into the joints, epidural space or around spinal nerves (called nerve root blocks).

- Medication to stop the progress of a systemic disease or to keep a disease in remission. (Systemic here means a disease process that is generalised throughout the body, causing damage to tissues.) Many cancer treatments and antibiotics fall into this group. Systemic diseases that affect the musculoskeletal system include rheumatoid arthritis, polymyalgia rheumatica, ankylosing spondylitis and gout. There are other less common ones. Most of these diseases are diagnosed following medical tests that confirm they are active. Disease-modifying anti-rheumatic drugs (DMARDs) are prescribed by specialists only for this group of conditions, and that is exactly what they can do – modify the disease. There have been huge advances in these treatments during the last 20 years.
- Medication that helps to reduce the risk of a condition developing, but is not intended to treat any symptoms. To the best of our knowledge, there are no examples specifically affecting the musculoskeletal system. Examples include statins, high blood pressure medication and aspirin, which are prescribed to reduce the risk of heart disease, kidney disease or stroke.

For the purposes of this chapter we will focus on the first group of medications, which are commonly prescribed for persistent back pain where there is no underlying systemic disease process. If you are in any doubt about your diagnosis, please check with your doctor.

The purpose of analgesic medication for persistent pain is to alleviate symptoms sufficiently to allow you to manage the functions of daily life. If it is not doing this then, quite simply, it is not working. These medications do not treat the underlying cause of the pain.

*It is helpful to understand that all pain-relieving medications can work for some people for a period of time but not everybody, and never all of the time.*

So let's look in more detail at the medication that is usually prescribed or purchased from pharmacies for persistent back pain.

## The anti-inflammatories

Medicines called ibuprofen, diclofenac and many others, both prescribed and purchased over the counter, fall into this group. The proper term is 'non-steroidal anti-inflammatory drugs' (NSAIDs).

Inflammation gets a bad press when it comes to pain. The process of inflammation is activated as soon as there is damage to a tissue caused by a sprain, tear, laceration, or a surgeon's knife. The chemicals released activate free nerve endings that fire danger-alert messages into the spinal cord (see chapter 3). These chemicals are essential because they trigger the body's natural healing processes. The inflammatory response usually only lasts a few days before the regenerative phase of healing takes over. The pain you feel is the brain's way of letting you know the tissue is in danger, to allow you to protect the vulnerable tissues while they are repaired. NSAIDs can be helpful to alleviate pain and are best used for a limited period of time. They are best for treating episodes of acute back pain.

The NSAID group of medicines have some unwanted side-effects when taken by mouth over a prolonged period of time. We don't mean to scare you, but these need to be recognised because they are common. They are:

- At the mild end of the spectrum, gastro-intestinal discomfort due to stomach and/or duodenal irritation and ulceration is an extremely common side-effect of NSAIDs. At least one in ten people who take NSAIDs regularly will experience these side-effects. More serious by far, and often unpredictable, is upper gastro-intestinal bleeding from the stomach or duodenum. People with this complication are usually very ill and need urgent admission to hospital, where some die despite the best of emergency care. Many doctors prescribe tablets that reduce (but cannot stop) this side-effect. These are known as proton pump inhibitors (PPIs); examples include omeprazole and lansoprazole. If they are prescribed, it is advisable to continue to take them for as long as you are using NSAIDs. They can be tapered off when NSAIDs are no longer being used.

- A less well-known but potentially very serious side-effect of regular use of NSAIDs is kidney disease. During the last two years we have seen several patients with persistent musculo-skeletal pain who had been taking NSAIDs regularly for over a year and who were manifesting early signs of kidney disease without realising it: these can include feeling more tired, having dry itchy skin, swelling of both feet and ankles, and puffiness around the eyes. Both were young and in otherwise good health. Once we recognised the problem, both patients chose to stop the NSAIDs and they both quickly felt a lot better.

- We are now beginning to realise that NSAIDs can contribute to the development of heart disease when taken over a long period of time. Some drugs in the group may be more hazardous than others, of course, but all might have this effect in vulnerable individuals.

- Research has also shown that the common headache can be made *worse* by regular use of NSAIDs – an example of a medication having the reverse of its intended effect when taken over the long term. How long? We can't be certain – it is not something that can easily be defined – but we are generally talking here of more than six weeks of regular use.

So, there are several unwanted effects with NSAIDs, particularly if they are taken for prolonged periods. Remember that when pain becomes persistent, it is more about the sensitivity of the nervous system and less about tissue damage or inflammation. So from the biological point of view it is illogical to use anti-inflammatories long term, as inflammation will only play a minor role, if any, in maintaining persistent pain. It will be a trade-off between the benefits they give you against unwanted side-effects both right now and in the future. Ultimately you must make that choice.

## Paracetamol

Properly known as acetaminophen, paracetamol is arguably the most reliable and effective analgesic available for common pain conditions in all age groups. Remarkably free of side-effects at recommended doses, it is very harmful in overdose. Limiting the number of paracetamol tablets that can be purchased in a pack over the counter has directly reduced the number of people being admitted to hospital and dying from paracetamol overdose.

Paracetamol is often blended with other drugs in one tablet; for example, co-codamol is paracetamol and codeine, while co-dydramol pairs it with dihydrocodeine, and there are other drugs that combine paracetamol with an anti-inflammatory.

As always, there are some drawbacks. Research is revealing that paracetamol taken over a long period of time can make headaches worse, just as with NSAIDs. Although to our knowledge no studies have yet shown this effect for back pain, it is wise to be cautious and accept that if it happens for headache, it could also happen for other regional pain problems.

Side-effects of paracetamol are rare but you should watch out for a rash or swelling as this might be indicative of an allergic reaction for which urgent medical attention must be sought.

Recent published research has also revealed that paracetamol taken for back pain is no more effective than taking a 'dummy' tablet, so its status as a reliable and effective analgesic is under challenge.

## The opioids

Everyone knows, or should know, how addictive morphine is. Addiction to strong opioids continues to ruin many lives and most of the bad press comes from illegal use. Less well known is that many of these opioids are prescribed by health professionals for persistent pain and users get stuck on them. In the USA, reliable data reveal that 15,000 deaths per year are linked to over-use of prescribed opioids and the same problem, on a lesser scale, is now occurring in the UK. Not such common knowledge is the fact that codeine and tramadol are also opioids. Codeine is classified as a 'weak' opioid and tramadol a 'moderately strong' opioid. Commonly prescribed 'strong' opioids include oxycodone, fentanyl and morphine preparations.

All opioids can ease pain for a short period of time, with the stronger opioids being more effective. The major downside is that tolerance quickly develops within a few weeks, meaning we need more of the drug to get the same effect. This applies to codeine too. Some people will be more vulnerable to this effect than others, but everyone will be affected. The brain's built-in neuro-chemical reward system will be hijacked sooner or later leading to habituation of the use of these drugs. To explain this further, we need to return to pain mechanism explained in chapters 3 and 4.

When you take an opioid, such as tramadol or co-codamol, you are giving yourself a dose of a chemical that can initially suppress your pain. This quickly tells the brain to expect reward from taking the substance. Your brain remembers this. Because you feel rewarded, your brain lays down new neural pathways to encourage you to repeat the use of it. Opioids release specific neurotransmitter chemicals much quicker than any other natural reward can, and the brain remembers this too, strengthening the pathways linked to needing further opioids. The problem is that over time, the original dosage gives less reward, so the dose needs to be raised to obtain the same effect. If the brain does not receive this reward, it alerts you that something is missing. It will do this by whatever means is necessary to get your attention: increase in pain intensity is the most obvious, but agitation is another. This drives you to take more tablets or use opioid patches, which deliver the drug through the skin. This convinces you, just enough, that the medicines are working. It is a subtle process and, like all addictions, the habit has a clever way of bypassing our conscious awareness. Even if we have an uneasy feeling that we are being drawn in to dependency, the brain has a way of suppressing these thoughts and convincing us that we are just fine. The brain can get addicted to anything that gives us satisfaction or pleasure. The list is long, and other than drugs includes work, alcohol, tobacco, shopping, exercise, sex, collecting things, taking risks (such as gambling), food ... and so on.

We do not believe in the concept of labelling people as having 'an addictive personality'. We can all develop addictions when the circumstances in our lives make us vulnerable. Once addicted, it can be very hard, but not impossible, to quit. Sadly, we have encountered people who have become addicted to prescribed strong opioids through no fault of their own and who have been unable to quit despite their best efforts and all the support and guidance we could offer.

Many people with persistent pain share with us their deep-held fears that they are addicted to the drugs that are prescribed for their pain, especially those containing codeine and tramadol. There's a general acceptance within society and the medical community that these drugs are harmless, but they are in denial. They are not harmless when they have hijacked your brain's reward system and thereby indirectly feed your persistent pain.

Those taking opioids for pain can experience other side-effects apart from addiction. There is a risk of accidental overdose and an increased risk of accidents, especially when driving. There is an increased risk of falls causing fracture, as well as depression and a lowered sex drive. Other common side-effects attributed to opioid use include nausea, vomiting, dizziness and constipation.

Even less well-known, but very important for people taking opioid medications for pain, is the effect called 'opioid-induced hyperalgesia'. Translated from medical jargon, this means that opioids are known to *increase* the sensitivity of the nervous system and therefore wind up the pain. You now understand how this will contribute to making pain worse in the longer term. We often see this effect in people referred to us for treatment. Do not despair if this is your situation, because the effect is reversible when the drugs are withdrawn – although it can take some people several months before their body eventually settles down following withdrawal.

## Anti-depressants and anti-epileptic drugs

These are widely prescribed to help alleviate pain, especially persistent pain. Examples in common use include amitriptyline, pregabalin and gabapentin. They are in a group of drugs that were developed for a separate purpose and have found an alternative use (aspirin has a similar history). It is worth knowing something about them if you are taking them or thinking of using them.

Amitriptyline has been around as a medication for over 60 years. It was developed initially as an anti-depressant drug but at high doses it was encumbered with side-effects that were common and often quite serious. About 40 years ago it was discovered that amitriptyline at very low doses has an analgesic effect on some types of pain, especially persistent pain. This effect has been extensively researched in many types of conditions and in many different settings. Doses as low as 5mg daily can be effective for some people.

Ironically, amitriptyline often gets a bad press. This is partly because it is classified as an anti-depressant and is only officially licensed for use in treating depression and bedwetting. But it has a useful side-effect that can be utilised when treating pain conditions: it is slightly sedative, so when taken at night can induce a better quality of sleep, something that is often lacking when pain is persistent. The best way of using amitriptyline is to start with as low a dose as possible – 10mg tablets – taken about two hours before you intend to sleep. Persevere each night because the benefit may not be noticeable for a number of days. After a week or so the dose can be adjusted upwards in small steps, according to its effectiveness, and trading this off against any unwanted effects.

It's worth trying it with an open mind to see for yourself. If you are not experiencing any benefit worth having by, say, two weeks minimum, four weeks maximum, then stop taking it. In any event, if it is helpful, view it as an aid to help you get going again and think about tailing it off after two or three months. It is not known to be addictive. It is unwise to use amitriptyline with other psychoactive drugs (meaning any that work on brain functioning) and in the UK it needs to be prescribed by a medical practitioner.

Gabapentin and pregabalin are anti-epileptic drugs that are also licensed for use in treating persistent pain, and pregabalin is also licensed for treating generalised anxiety disorders. As with all medications, give them a trial run by all means but if they are not helping to ease symptoms enough to get you going and improve function within eight to twelve weeks then they are unlikely to help you in the long term.

## So should I take medication?

We would suggest the best starting point is to discuss medication use with your doctor. As a general rule, if he or she thinks a course of treatment is appropriate, agree to a trial run with a review after six to eight weeks to assess whether you feel it is benefiting you. Even if the treatment is benefiting you, it is still helpful to arrange a regular review with your doctor to ensure taking drugs in the medium and longer term is not affecting your overall health. If they are not benefiting you, you can discuss alternative options with your doctor, or seek alternative help with your pain. We would recommend accessing a combined physical and psychological rehabilitation programme, such as the one described in this book.

We have looked at the potential benefits and drawbacks of using medication for persistent back pain, but this leaves some unanswered questions. We've tried to address a couple of them below.

☞ If these drugs are unlikely to be effective in the long term then why am I given them on repeat prescription?

This is a question we are often asked and the answer is complex.

Despite emerging evidence questioning the use of medication for pain over the long term, national guidelines for medical practitioners recommend their use. General practitioners usually have little else they can offer other than a prescription when you are in pain so they issue it with the best of intentions. Following up these prescriptions is often overlooked and sometimes people are simply given repeat prescriptions if they request more.

Doctors in general practice don't have time to discuss the complexities of persistent pain. It's a complicated business and they often have only a few minutes for each appointment. Meanwhile there is an expectation among patients that when they go and see the doctor, they will emerge with something for their pain; the easiest and quickest thing to do is to prescribe medication. Doctors may not have the option of referring you to a service that will help you look at your persistent pain from a wider perspective, so they do their best with the limited time and resources they have available. Providing a repeat prescription is the quickest and easiest thing to do.

Over the past few years there have been increasing numbers of published research papers and leading articles in medical journals bringing these problems to the greater awareness of health professionals, so we hope this wider understanding will lead to more care being taken with the prescription of analgesics.

> ☞ I think I might be addicted to my medication. How do I come off it?

Another common question we are asked.

Firstly, it really does help to acknowledge the fact that addiction is established. It is not something to be ashamed of: neither you nor the doctors who prescribed the pills set out with the intention of creating this problem. There is no place for guilt, anger or blame. You have a choice, as always.

Many people list tapering off their medication as one of the goals in their recovery plan. This is a very powerful goal as it shows they are ready to commit to making changes to improve their health status. Tapering off medication is best done while you are applying the other principles outlined in this book. It is vitally important to replace medication with something more rewarding, such as graded exercise, relaxation or engaging in enjoyable activities. As soon as the brain is rewarded with a more pleasurable activity it will quickly want more, and the motivation to continue will be much easier to find. The hardest part, of course, is making a start.

As with all plans, it helps to identify obstacles, barriers and pitfalls to achieving the goal. Make a list if it helps. Planning ahead means you are much more likely to succeed. You may want to revisit the chapter on goal setting to help you with this. Consult your doctor about any change in medication, and ask him or her to help you to structure a medication reduction plan. They are unlikely to refuse.

It can be difficult to reduce the dose of medication when it comes as a single tablet or patch. In this case you can either chop up a tablet into smaller chunks, if it will go, cut a patch down in size – or ask your GP to prescribe a different formulation to help you reduce the dosage in stages.

Plan in advance how you are going to deal with withdrawal symptoms. Don't ignore the possibility or you run a high risk of failing. Some doctors will prescribe another less addictive substance, and this *can* help when trying to come off strong opioids. However, for most people and for most analgesics this is not necessary and might even make matters worse. Within 12 to 36 hours of reducing the dose of opioids, expect your pain volume dial to be turned up. This is normal and will usually pass within a short space of time.

Ask family and close friends to be patient with you and support you, especially if you behave in ways that are uncharacteristic – for example, if you experience mood swings. Be patient; they will pass. It helps to plan an activity to distract attention from how you are feeling. Craft projects, such as embroidery, knitting, woodwork and photography, are excellent. Some people have told us they did a large jigsaw puzzle to help them get through this phase. Like craft work, jigsaws can be done in short bursts and left incomplete then taken up again later until the job is finished. These methods are more likely to succeed than sitting watching TV (which is too passive for the brain) or allowing the mind to dwell on your symptoms and monitoring them moment by moment.

Another tip for breaking the habit is to change the location where you keep the medication. If you make it more difficult to access the pills, or gather up those you will not be needing and take them back to the pharmacy, it will help to reinforce the message to your brain that 'you will no longer be needing them'.

Plan for pitfalls. The most obvious here is relapse. On balance of probability, it will occur. Don't be hard on yourself or beat yourself up if it happens. This is guaranteed to make you feel worse by raising your stress levels. It's better to reflect on the reasons for the relapse.

- Have you tried to reduce your medication too fast (the most common reason)?

- Have you not been able to distract yourself from distressing symptoms? Revise the plan and try something different next time.
- Do you really want to withdraw from this medication or is there some deep-seated feeling that you still need it?

Most people we see who plan reduction and withdrawal of analgesic medication using this approach do succeed and are rewarded for their efforts. However, despite everyone's best efforts it can be really difficult for some people to withdraw from strong opioids when they have been using them for a long time. For these folk, it might be best to acknowledge the situation, discuss it with their medical advisor and agree to remain on the lowest dose manageable, while at the same time learning other methods to help yourself as outlined in this book. Avoid the temptation to escalate use of strong opioids during flare-ups, but don't try to reduce dosage or stop altogether when pain is bad. Try again at some time in the future.

Some people we see choose to withdraw from analgesic medication by stopping the lot all at once, or at least stopping each one abruptly in turn. That is their choice and if they prefer to do things that way, then fine. However, if you do this you must plan for the withdrawal bounce they call 'cold turkey'. We have worked with many people who have been through this and it can succeed but it will probably mean a very tough few days. Make sure you inform your doctor (and those closest to you) that you are going to do this, as there can be significant side-effects as you withdraw, including fever, sweats, aching joints, agitation, anxiety and poor sleep.

The best method for most people, and certainly the only method for withdrawal from very strong opioids, is a step-down method. For very strong opioids, such as morphine, it can take between one month and two years. For all other medications in this category, one to six weeks is a guide. During this time, set short-term goals for reducing the dose in a gradual way as outlined in chapter 5; for example, step down one dose per day every two, five or seven days, gradually tapering off. It will pay to set goals and aim to stick to them, revising the plan if you are progressing too fast or too slow.

## Going forward

The aim of this section is to give you guidance on how to get the best out of medication and how to reduce its use *if you choose to do so*. Don't feel as though you must. As you learn the other techniques for managing persistent pain, outlined in later chapters of this book, you might find you simply don't need as much pain relief as you used to. We'll start in the next chapter by looking at ways to help you move more freely.

# CHAPTER 8

# MOVING WITH FREEDOM AND CONFIDENCE

When back pain persists, it affects how freely and confidently we move. We notice that people develop cautious and adapted movement patterns as they learn protective ways of moving in response to their pain. Normal daily activities – such as moving from sitting to standing, getting on and off the floor, bending down to pick something up and stepping upwards – can become difficult due to the presence of persistent back pain. This makes engaging in daily life difficult and can be deeply frustrating. Remember: we now know that changes occur in the body map in your brain, and that the neural circuits supplying the muscles stop firing if we don't use them; they become redundant, and those intricate patterns of normal movement become even more problematic for us. But we also know that these neural networks and patterns are adaptable and can be retrained with time, practice and effort.

In this chapter we will help you to move with freedom and confidence again, and this will involve exercise.

It is interesting to note that despite many research trials on different types of approach to back pain, no particular type of exercise has been proven more effective than others. Huge sums of research money have been spent trying to find a magic set of exercises that can alleviate back pain, but none has proven any more successful. Sometimes, certain exercise approaches will be heavily promoted in the media, and marketed by commercial organisations. For a while they might become the latest buzz word in back pain management, but none has been proven to provide a solution for every single person with back problems when tested in high-quality research trials.

However, virtually every clinical guideline relating to back pain promotes exercise as a high-priority treatment. So the natural conclusion is that you should just get moving, no matter how you do it. This might involve going to the gym, going for a walk, joining an aqua-aerobics class or doing yoga. All types of exercise are helpful for back pain, so long as they are started gradually, at a low level initially, and progressively increased over time. If you have already found an exercise approach that works well for you, stick with it; it is getting you moving and helping you to function. If you haven't, maybe some ideas in this chapter will inspire you.

## Won't I risk damaging my back if I exercise?

One common problem we come across when we show people how to move with freedom and confidence is that they have been told to be careful with their backs, and that only certain types of exercise are safe. But it is important to remember that the spine is a strong and robust structure, designed to manage all sorts of physical stresses and strains. It maintains its strength and stamina through regular use, so functional exercises, such as those described on pages 122-8, are often the best type of exercise to help restore function. The human spine has had millions of years to evolve and our ancestors survived well enough to pass on their genes without being over-careful about how they moved.

Research informs us that *prolonged* heavy lifting, twisting and bending or static postures over a *sustained* period of time can increase the frequency of back pain. It seems to be the same in all societies and cultures. *Disability* due to back pain is something different, however, and this has reached epidemic levels in industrialised societies. So if you are thinking of building up your activity levels following a period of prolonged disability, you need to be sensible that you don't push yourself too hard, particularly to begin with. If you pace yourself, take regular breaks and build up activity gradually, you will start to notice improvements.

We have already talked about how fear of certain movements can be an obstacle to recovering function, so if you are worried about what exercise might do to your back, or worried it may damage your back, the best way to test it out is to try some simple low-level exercises to begin with. Don't charge into this like a bull at a gate; start slowly and progress gradually and remember it is highly unlikely that movement and exercise initially at low levels, and built up gradually, will cause long-term damage to your back.

Also, be aware that if you haven't exercised much for a prolonged period of time, your cardiovascular fitness (the ability of your heart and lungs to supply oxygen to your muscles) has probably suffered and you are likely to feel very tired and possibly breathless at first. This is normal, and not a reason to stop. In time you should find that these symptoms ease.

When you notice the exercises becoming easier, you can increase the number of repetitions or adapt the exercises to include regular movements and postures that you would like to become a part of your day-to-day life. We strongly encourage our patients to try any common everyday activity as an exercise first. Then, if your occupation involves particular movements or postures – such as climbing stairs, bending down to load a dishwasher, or moving from sitting to standing – you can adapt your exercise routine to incorporate them. Remember that in doing this, you are strengthening the pathways between the nervous system and the muscles, and that with repetition those pathways rewire themselves and become stronger. In this way, your physical strength will improve too.

# What sort of exercise should I do?

If you have avoided exercising for a prolonged period of time, we recommend you do a mixture of gentle exercises, including cardiovascular, stretching and strengthening exercises. Remember as you do them that movement is not harmful. It might feel uncomfortable at first but find a pace and a level you can manage and keep it up. Consistency is key.

## Cardiovascular exercise

As your cardiovascular fitness, also known as endurance or aerobic fitness, has probably diminished after a period of prolonged inactivity, it is advisable to build this up again. The best way to make a start is to set yourself a walking programme. This does not require special shoes or equipment, gym membership or swimming pool costs. If you need to, refer back to the graded activity principles on pages 85-6 in chapter 6.

Think of a suitable walking route you could start doing regularly – it may be round a local park, or a walk to your local shop. Time yourself completing this walk, and over time aim to gradually increase the speed you walk at. Over a period of six to eight weeks you will be able to do it faster. Once you have achieved this you may want to get more adventurous and plan a walk in the countryside. The further you walk, the more your cardiovascular fitness will improve. Your back might feel worse to begin with, but this is not a sign that you are damaging yourself; it's just the muscles getting used to activity again.

If you like a gym environment, you could work on your cardiovascular fitness on a cross trainer, rowing machine or an exercise bike. Have a fitness assessment with a qualified trainer before you start and ask him or her to help you design a progressive programme. Again, find a comfortable starting point, and grade up activity gradually. Expect to feel tired, and be aware that you might experience more pain to begin with, but stick to the plan and increase activity in a step-by-step manner.

To gain the maximum health benefits from cardiovascular exercise, guidelines suggest you should aim to do 150 minutes of moderately vigorous exercise per week. You could set this as a long-term goal, something to try and achieve within a period of two or three months perhaps. It may sound like a tall order to begin with, but using a graded approach will make it easier to achieve. Regular exercise will stimulate the release of feel-good endorphins into your bloodstream and in time will help to turn the volume down on your back pain.

## Stretching

Physical inactivity will result in shorter, tighter muscles. If muscles are not stretched out regularly, they tend to contract and this is likely to be one of a number of factors contributing to the stiffness that you feel in the part of your body that has been in pain. Have a look at chapter 4, page 53, to remind yourself what happens to your muscles when pain persists.

There are varying opinions on the best way to stretch, but remember that pain is a protective response – it will encourage you to guard against moving too much. This may well be helpful when you have a new injury, as it protects the area that needs to heal, but when pain is persistent, this protective response has outlived its usefulness.

Most people tell us that slower stretching movements, in which they coordinate the movement with their breathing, are most helpful. This is the method that has been taught by yoga experts for many centuries. A slow, sustained stretch over five to ten seconds is a good rule of thumb to begin with, but you will be able to lengthen this period of time as you continue.

When people have been in pain for a long time we invariably see them holding their breath as they try and push themselves through discomfort. Very few people realise they are doing it until it is pointed out (like so many habits). You break the habit by concentrating on breathing at the same time as stretching. It seems intuitive to breathe *in* on any movement where the body rises, for example getting out of a chair, and to breathe *out* as the body goes down, for example sitting down in a chair. Practise and find out what works best for you. It does not matter provided that you breathe with the movement and learn to stop holding your breath. Breathing out will release tension from the body in an instant. With practice it starts to become natural, and that's when movements start to feel enjoyable and easier again.

Some stretches we recommend are illustrated on pages 117-22. It's a good idea to stretch both before and after an exercise session and we coach everyone we work with to get into the habit of stretching combined with breathing control at intervals during every day. There are opportunities in everyone's schedule for a little stretching. It all adds up. Shorter periods of activity might work best for those who, for a variety of reasons, do not find it easy to set aside longer periods for exercise.

## Recommended exercises

It is normal to feel *some* pain when doing the following exercises. This will ease as you repeat them over a period of a few weeks, as your body becomes conditioned to the exercise. Remember that if you have persistent back pain, you will not be damaging yourself. But if you experience increasing pain as you exercise, which does not settle or gets significantly worse after exercising, you are wise to cease that specific exercise.

We recommend that readers use graded activity principles to judge how many repetitions to do. If after ten repetitions, for example, you feel moderate discomfort in your thighs and back, this is to be expected. You can increase the number of repetitions as the exercise becomes easier.

Try each of the following exercises, find out what you can manage without too much discomfort, then set yourself goals to improve over time.

## Back stretch

Get down on the floor on all fours. Keeping your hands on the floor, breathe out slowly as you sit back on your heels, feeling the stretch through your lower back. Keep your head down between your upper arms as you feel the stretch.

## Rotation in lying

Lie on your back with your knees bent and feet on the floor, resting your arms by your sides. Breathe out and roll your knees slowly to the left. Breathe in, then breathe out again as you roll them to the right.

## *Lateral flexion*

Stand with your feet hip-width apart and arms by your sides. Breathe out as you reach down your right side, pushing your hand down your leg. Stand up again then reach down the left side, breathing out.

## Spinal extension

Stand in front of a doorway or wall. Rest your hands on the doorframe or wall, making a V shape. Breathing out, reach upwards with your hands, feeling the stretch in your back.

## Bending forwards

Stand with your feet hip-width apart and arms by your sides. Breathing out, bend your back and reach downwards. Go as far as you can then return to starting position. Keep your knees soft and slightly bent when bending forwards.

## Deep squat

Stand in front of a stable piece of furniture with your feet flat on the floor. Hold onto it with your hands at around waist height, and slowly squat down, breathing out and keeping your heels on the floor. Feel the stretch in your back and let it flex, don't hold it straight.

## Functional exercise – endurance and coordination

Many everyday activities that you have been avoiding because of your persistent back pain are suitable to include as part of your recovery exercise plan. The principles of graded activity remain the same. You just need to start at a low level and build up gradually. As you manage more over time, your strength and coordination will gradually improve. The exercises below move the body in many different directions, and will help you to regain flexibility and confidence.

Again, remember that you may feel worse as you start to do these exercises. Begin with just a few repetitions and build up when you are ready. To improve your endurance, it is best to do regular repetitions, spending just two minutes on each exercise at first, and then gradually build up the amount of time when you are able.

## Sit to stand

Sit in a chair with your feet on the floor and arms crossed over your chest. Bend forwards until your head is above your knees then push down into your legs and raise yourself up to standing position. If you find this difficult, start from a higher chair or other surface first then slowly choose lower seats as it gets easier. Sit down again and repeat.

## Step-ups

You can do this exercise using the bottom step of the stairs, if you don't have an exercise step like the one shown in the picture. Step up with one foot then bring the other up alongside it then step down again. Swap so that you lead with the opposite foot next time and repeat. If step-ups feel too difficult to begin with, choose a lower step then gradually increase the height over time.

## Bending and lifting from standing

Start by placing an object on a low chair. Stand in front of the chair, bend your knees, hips and back forwards, pick up the object then return to standing. The key lies in bending the whole of your spine, rather than keeping it braced straight. We're against bracing! When you can manage this lift easily, try placing the object on a step and bending to lift it from there. Finally, try to lift an object from the floor using the same method.

## Balancing on one leg

Stand and lift each leg off the floor in turn, seeing how long you can keep your balance. As you get better at this, practise doing it with your eyes closed, which is *much* harder.

## *Walking with light weights*

If you don't have any gym-type weights at home, you could try holding a can of tomatoes or a water bottle in either hand. Move your arms back and forwards as you walk around. Increase the weight carried if you find it easy.

## Sitting and twisting

A Swiss exercise ball such as the one shown in the pictures is ideal, but if you don't have one, use a chair without arms. Sit with your feet on the floor and your arms curved in front of you at chest height, fingers balanced on top of the opposite hand. Breathing out, turn your upper body to the right while keeping your feet on the floor. Breathe in, then breathe out as you turn your upper body to the left.

## Spinal extension

Stand in front of a step. As you step up onto it, reach upwards with both arms, feeling your spine stretching. Repeat, leading with the opposite foot next time.

# Planning exercise towards your goal

If you are planning to go back to work, or to return to a sport or hobby you have been avoiding, graded functional exercise is a good way to manage your recovery. It is helpful to think about all the component parts of the activity you want to return to and build these into a graded exercise plan just as Pete did in the story on page 64.

Let's take the example of golf. The thought of playing a full round of golf with no preparation might seem overwhelming and unachievable, but if you break it down into a few component parts it can be done step by step. Remember this is how Pete returned to playing tennis in chapter 5. Here are the actions you will have to manage to get back to golf:

- Walking regularly for distances of no more than 200 yards
- Bending down to place your ball on the tee and picking it up out of the hole
- Twisting and flexing your spine as in the golf swing you use to tee off
- Hacking your way through the rough, on uneven ground, in search of your ball
- Hitting the ball at an odd angle in a tough bunker

So, an exercise regime to help you prepare to return to playing golf might involve:

- Taking regular short walks, and building your tolerance for walking
- Bending your knees and your back to put something down on the floor then pick it up again
- Going to the driving range, and practising a half swing, with a small basket of balls. Build up to a three-quarter swing and then a full swing over the course of a few practice sessions
- Walk over some rough ground for short distances
- Practise sitting for increasing periods of time, ensuring you get up and move around regularly
- Play nine holes on a short course once you feel ready

In this way you can use a graded exercise plan to allow you to take a stepped exercise approach to recovery.

What goals did you set for yourself in chapter 5? Think about how you could plan an exercise programme to help you achieve them.

- What movements do you need to improve to do the activity?
- What level of endurance will you need?

- How can you recreate the component parts of the activity?
- When you feel ready to try the activity, what is the best starting point?

Using your own personal exercise plan could make it easier to achieve some of your targets than you previously imagined.

### Delivering the mail

Mohammed was a postman who was experiencing persistent low back pain which affected his ability to do his usual postal round. He was struggling with the bending and twisting associated with unloading and loading his mail van, then carrying the mailbag round with him on his usual walking route. He was having to take intermittent days off work due to back pain and was finding it difficult to fulfil his duties. He noticed he was tensing up as he moved, and he certainly looked very cautious when we watched him exercising in the gym. He acknowledged he had become fearful of particular types of movement and was instinctively avoiding them. Mohammed was keen to be able to continue his work and all the duties it entailed.

Once Mohammed accepted that it was safe to exercise, even though he was apprehensive to begin with, he made a start on some functional exercises we advised him to try.

He was clearly struggling to lift things from the floor, so instead he lifted a 1kg ball from a chair. This was easier. When it was pointed out to Mohammed that he was holding his breath while lifting the ball, he agreed to see what difference breathing as he moved would make. He chose to breathe out as he lowered the ball and breathe in as he lifted. To begin with he emphasised the breath sound: it could be heard around the room – but that didn't matter. Within a few minutes, he was able to move further and more comfortably. Others around him remarked that he looked more relaxed and he was no longer going red in the face and neck when lifting and bending. He agreed to practise this new routine for two or three minutes at a time, six times a day, over the next few days.

Within a week he noticed his confidence when bending was improving: he was able to lift the 1kg ball from the floor to chest height and replace it nice and slowly, repeating for two to three minutes. He was also beginning to allow the whole of his spine to bend in a curve rather than keeping it braced straight and bending from the hips and knees as previously. This, he remarked, flew in the face of all that he had been told to do on his training courses as a postman. (Interestingly, recent research has established that 'manual handling training', a legal health and safety requirement in the UK, does not reduce the incidence of back pain, or the level of disability associated with back pain, when compared with doing nothing or doing something else.) Mohammed then progressed to lifting small weights from the floor. He said he felt as if he was relearning how to lift and bend, something he used to do without a thought. This was the case: his nervous system was being rewired as he relearned patterns of movement that had been trained into him as he was growing up.

As Mohammed's confidence grew, he added in some of his own exercises, which matched the types of activities he needed to do at work. It was not long before he was handling a simulated postbag in the gym.

He continued with these exercises for several weeks, to the point when he no longer needed to do them, as he had restored his function to previous levels. At that stage he returned to his normal daily work routine. He really enjoyed getting out walking on his round again, an aspect of the job that made it all worthwhile. He soon forgot about the short-term discomfort he experienced when he first started those functional exercises.

Mohammed was pleased to share with others on the same recovery programme that changing his breathing pattern during movement was the key to his remarkable progress.

## In summary

To move with freedom and confidence, remember these messages:

- Movement won't cause damage to your back, even though it may hurt initially.
- There is no one magic exercise approach that works for everyone – you need to find a way that works for you and stick with it.
- Combine cardiovascular (aerobic) exercise with stretching and strength/coordination exercises.
- Breathe through the movement; break the habit of holding your breath when moving.
- Decide what you want to be doing more of, and base your exercise plan around this.
- Keep on repeating movements to rewire those neural connections that have become redundant through lack of use. The muscles love exercise: they thrive on it!
- Make sure you enjoy doing the exercises you choose so you are more likely to continue in the long term.

# CHAPTER 9

# LEARNING WAYS TO RELAX EFFECTIVELY

I n the busy modern world, few of us prioritise making time for recuperation. Having enough 'down-time' and good-quality sleep is important for everyone, but even more so when you are living with the constant stress and strain of persistent back pain and its many knock-on effects.

When we first see people with persistent back pain, we often ask them a simple question: 'What do you do to help yourself relax and switch off?'

The response is usually: 'Nothing', 'I don't know how to relax', 'I can't relax' or 'I haven't got time for that with all I have on my plate.'

Another question we ask is: 'Describe the *quality* of sleep you generally have.'

The responses are almost always 'Awful', 'Can't remember the last time I woke up feeling refreshed', and so forth.

We all know how important enough rest is. We all know that when we get tired we often become irritable, moody, make silly mistakes or find it difficult to make decisions. People with back pain will recognise that their symptoms are worse when they are not sleeping well. In fact, there is an inverse relationship between pain intensity and sleep quality: as sleep quality improves, pain decreases; as sleep quality deteriorates, pain increases. This is obvious, so it is incredible that we still neglect this critically important area of our health.

The three levels of recuperation we will discuss in this chapter are rest, relaxation and sleep.

## Rest

Resting means stopping for a period of time each day to escape work tasks, cast off stress, and unwind. It is about switching the focus of our attention. In good health, the brain is incredibly efficient at focusing attention for periods of about 90 minutes. After that it needs a break, and short breaks can be very effective. A walk to another room, a chat with a work colleague or staring out of the window for a minute or two (especially if our task involves working with display equipment and screens) can all do the trick.

When we are under stress, when our backs are hurting more than usual, or when we are taking analgesic or psycho-active medication, the brain's ability to focus is significantly diminished. At these times it is even more important to plan short breaks from the task in hand. Taking a lunch break away from our desks is helpful and we find it sad that so many people feel they cannot do this in their workplace. And it's not just office workers who are vulnerable. People who work from home, including those in caring or nurturing roles, are arguably much more prone to neglecting time for rest breaks. Some just keep going until they collapse with exhaustion. A few of us drive ourselves to burn-out in the hope that the annual holiday will rectify everything. It is very common for us to hear about this pattern of behaviour in people with persistent back pain. It is a habit that needs to be changed if you are going to recover.

Neglecting the need for short breaks comes at a cost over time: diminished efficiency, stress symptoms, sleep disturbance, worsening pain, and so on. The evenings are, for most people, a time for rest. This time needs to be set aside for rest but it is easy to fill it with tasks on an ever-expanding 'to-do' list.

For some people, activities normally associated with taking time out for rest and recuperation, such as exercise in a gym or a group class, becomes a chore, a 'have to' or 'must do' task. If this is the case then it will most likely become counter-productive; it may well wind up your pain intensity and delay your recovery. Building periods of rest into your week is an essential part of your pathway to recovery plan.

## Relaxation

Scientific research supports what many people intuitively know: we relax when we are doing something we enjoy that absorbs our attention. Here are some examples:

- Satisfying hobbies
- *Pleasurable* physical exercise
- Creative craft work
- Gardening
- Reading a good book
- Listening to music
- Playing music
- Singing
- Stroking or exercising a pet
- A good conversation
- Solving puzzles
- Fun and laughter

No doubt, you can think of more. Watching TV and playing computer games or any kind of screen activity is not included in this list because such activities are known to maintain or induce even higher levels of physiological stress arousal. This may come as a surprise to some. Watching TV before bed, or even having a TV in the bedroom, is known to promote poorer-quality sleep. We do not fully understand the reasons why this is at present.

When it comes to resting and relaxing, the key is to find out what works best for you, making sure you ring-fence time to do it, then sticking to it. Finding the balance between work, rest and relaxation is a challenge all of us face and, of course, as life circumstances change, so too does our need to re-evaluate our rest and relaxation and make changes where necessary.

## Stimulate your relaxation response

Taking time out of the day to relax *actively* and to wind down the nervous system will help you gain more control of your back pain. You will also discover many other benefits. When doing this you are activating the parasympathetic nervous system, which triggers the winding-down of those danger-alert messages we talked about in chapter 3. You are stimulating nature's analgesic pathway and the more you practise, the better you get at it and the more benefit you will derive as neural connections are strengthened.

Active relaxation is easy to learn and put into practice. You do not have to invest time in learning new hobbies or going to classes. You do not have to change your lifestyle if you choose not to. You do, however, consciously need to make some time to practise the relaxation skill you choose. Like everything else we learn, we need to practise it until it becomes natural.

The rewards are massive. You will learn how to turn down the pain in your body, and how to shift your attention away from worrying or catastrophising thoughts. It will help you nip a flare-up of pain in the bud before it takes over your life. It is free and comes with no side-effects. We teach these skills on every course. When we ask people what has helped them most at the end of our programmes, by far the most common response is the technique of 7:11 breathing (see below). Even years later, we are told that it is this skill that proved most effective over time.

## 7:11 breathing method

7:11 breathing is a form of diaphragmatic breathing in which the out-breath is longer than the in-breath. When you are breathing with the diaphragm, you are using the full extent of the lungs. It can be done in any position – sitting, standing, lying down. If you are lying down, an onlooker can see that the belly rises more than the chest.

As you breathe in to a count of 7, the diaphragm muscle moves down and the belly bulges outwards. You then count to 11 while breathing out and the belly goes down. Any rhythm in which the out-breath lasts longer than the in-breath will do, but we call this method 7:11 because it rhymes and is easy to remember.

It is highly effective at calming people down because the out-breaths stimulate the parasympathetic nervous system and trigger a relaxation response: blood pressure goes down, the pupils dilate, the heart rate slows and emotional arousal goes down, allowing more clear and logical thinking. Visualise a control panel inside the brain where the technicians are turning down the dials that control pain intensity, like a dimmer switch; or try any other visualisation that appeals to you.

When you are first learning the 7:11 technique, and when you are practising for more than five minutes, find a comfortable position in your favourite reclining chair or lie supine or semi-supine on a mat.

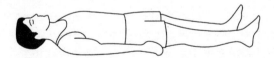

Supine (see above) means lying flat on your back with your head aligned with your spine – or use a very small cushion to support your head. Place your arms by your sides, palms facing up, feet flopping out. The semi-supine position (see below) is the same except that the knees are bent and the soles of the feet are flat on the ground. A few cushions placed under the knees may make this position more comfortable. The priority is finding the most comfortable position for you. Choose a position in which the main muscles that support us when we are standing upright (i.e. those most prone to tension in pain disorders) are able to relax properly.

Many find it helpful to place one hand on the belly and one hand on the upper chest, or both hands on the belly with fingertips touching at the extreme out-breath, when the belly is lowest. This helps you to monitor the movement of the chest and belly and gives tactile feedback on how you are doing, which is especially helpful when learning the practice.

- Choose a place where you are not going to be disturbed. Switch phones to silent.
- Start by doing 5 minutes twice a day and build up to 20 or 30 minutes for maximum benefit.
- Concentrate and aim to focus all of your attention on your breathing and counting. Breathe in to the count of 7 and out to the count of 11. Your mind will inevitably wander off – that's normal. Be patient with yourself, accept it happens and gently allow the focus of your attention to come back to the breathing, the movement of your belly and the counting.

As with all skills, practice brings success so be patient with yourself as you are learning. If you are in pain and have been for a long time, or are feeling very tense and stressed, we recommend practising 7:11 breathing for about 30 minutes twice a day to train the nervous system to turn down its hyper-arousal state. Remember that while you are practising, the nervous system is 'rewiring' itself – or, if you prefer to think in software jargon, 're-booting' itself. There is active healing going on. And the deeper relaxation allows blood to flow more easily into those chronically tight and oversensitive muscles that contribute to your pain.

At first some people find it difficult to allow the belly to distend during the in-breath. This is probably because of years of habitual holding in of the stomach either subconsciously (nobody wants a 'sagging' belly) or consciously because you were following the instruction of some methods of movement control.

When you get better at it you will begin to notice that you can calm down more quickly with maybe 3 to 5 minutes of 7:11 breathing. This can be done almost anywhere – say standing waiting for transport or in a queue. It can also be very helpful to induce sleep.

Needless to say, you should not practise when you are at the controls of a moving motor vehicle or operating machinery.

## The fist-clenching method

This is an alternative method of inducing the relaxation response, which some people prefer. It is based on the fact that muscles relax more easily after they have first been actively tensed. You can start with any muscle group in the body. The method we teach, arguably the easiest to learn, begins with the fists. It is suitable for everyone except those who have problems with their fingers, wrist joints or tendons or suffer from carpal tunnel syndrome. If you have long fingernails you may want to cut them before you use this method. If you have problems with your hands then you could try this method while focusing on facial muscles.

- Find a comfortable position to start. This method can work very well standing up.

- Clench both hands to make tight fists. Focus all of your attention on the fists and gradually build up the tension over several minutes. Really focus. Feel the fingernails digging into the skin of the palms, feel the thumb squeezing the index finger, feel the skin stretch over the knuckles, feel the tension increasing around the wrists and beginning to spread up the arms. Really concentrate on building up and maintaining the tension. Notice any change in the temperature of the hands and wrists.
- After a few minutes of this concentrated tension, count down from 5 to 1 and when you get to 1 – *let go*. Let go of all the tension and effort. Notice the changing sensations in the hands, wrists and forearms. Pay attention to the changes in temperature, tingling, heaviness or any other sensations. Notice the feeling of relaxation that is now present and simply allow that relaxation to spread up the arms, around the neck, to the facial muscles, chest, stomach, back, buttocks and all the way down to the feet.
- Allow time for this relaxation to spread around the body; do not hurry it.
- During this phase you can do some visualisation practice if you choose; for example, visualise a wave of healing going around the body and reaching all of those areas that need to relax more.

## Sleep

Sleep is an entirely natural process, one that we didn't even have to think about when we were babies or infants. However, busy adult lives and persistent pain can raise our levels of stress so high that we have difficulty sleeping well. At night our brains don't switch off but can stimulate us into mental activity, whether problem solving, list making or anxious imagination. We do all sorts of things to 'try' to get to sleep, rather than getting our conscious minds 'out of the way' so that we can allow sleep to take over. In this section we aim to show you some sleep-hygiene techniques that will aid natural and restful sleep.

Many of the difficulties we regularly experience in life – including difficulty in sleeping – arise from patterns of thinking and habits we have learned, whether unintentionally or consciously. For example, we may regularly postpone going to bed because we are channel-hopping on TV, playing computer games, surfing the Internet or chatting on social media. If sleep has become problematic, we may dread getting ready for bed, already anxious about whether we will be able to sleep. Sleeping becomes not about 'switching off' the brain in these cases, but rather activating it in a different way.

Using a sleep-hygiene approach will start to change unhelpful patterns and stimulate thinking and activities which pave the way for a good night's sleep.

Here is what to do:

- For an hour before bedtime, avoid screens. Watching TV, playing computer games and surfing the Internet are all too stimulating.
- Minimise persistent worrying by keeping a notebook of worry 'topics'. Every time a worry comes into your head write it down. This can help you to make better sense of your worry and you may realise when you put it into words that it is not worth worrying about at all.
- Plan a set routine around bedtime and getting-up time.
- If you wake in the night, avoid turning on the light or looking at the time. Try 7:11 breathing or another relaxation technique.
- If you don't get back to sleep within about 30 minutes, get up and sit in a cool, dark room. Do not do something you enjoy. As soon as you are really tired, leave the task and return to bed then focus on a breathing or relaxation technique again.
- If you are still awake after another 20 to 30 minutes, get up and do another boring task or pick up on the one you left. Once your brain realises that it will be punished for not sleeping

(rather than rewarded) it will learn to get you off to sleep at night.

- You may also need to address physical factors that might be affecting your sleep: alcohol, caffeine, tobacco, and eating or exercising late can cause disturbed sleep, as can hormonal imbalances and a bedroom that is either too hot or too cold.
- Make your bedroom a place you associate with sleep. If possible, remove the TV, computer, office or studying equipment to another room. Bedtime reading might be better done in another room.
- Consider wearing a mask over your eyes if there is too much background light, or install black-out blinds. Earplugs might help if sounds (such as another person snoring) disturb you.

The more practised you become at relaxing, the more easily you will drift off to sleep and the deeper your sleep will be.

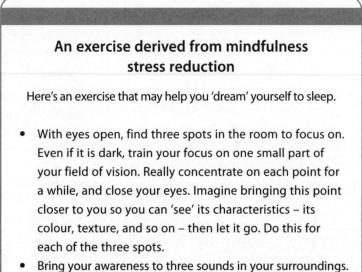

### An exercise derived from mindfulness stress reduction

Here's an exercise that may help you 'dream' yourself to sleep.

- With eyes open, find three spots in the room to focus on. Even if it is dark, train your focus on one small part of your field of vision. Really concentrate on each point for a while, and close your eyes. Imagine bringing this point closer to you so you can 'see' its characteristics – its colour, texture, and so on – then let it go. Do this for each of the three spots.
- Bring your awareness to three sounds in your surroundings. These might include sounds outside or inside the room, or even sounds inside your body, such as breathing. Spend a few moments focusing on each, then let them go.

- Bring your awareness to three feelings. These might include the warmth or weight of the bed covers on your body, the air on your face or an internal sensation. Focus on each in turn and then let them go.
- Now imagine three relaxing or absorbing scenes – such as a tranquil lake, a colourful parade, a sunset. Stay with each of your imagined scenes for a few moments.
- Next imagine three relaxing or absorbing sounds – a piece of music, the hiss of a steam train, a waterfall. Stay with these sounds for a few moments.
- Next imagine three pleasing sensations – walking across soft grass, skiing on fresh snow, plunging into a warm pool. Stay with these feelings in turn for a while.

Continue to switch between imagining three new, relaxing sights, three new sounds and three new sensations until you drift off to sleep.

Any changes you make will help to promote activity in your body's natural analgesic pathway, reducing the intrusive nature of persistent pain and allowing you to move and sleep more comfortably. Your body's immune system and ability to heal itself will function better when you are getting the rest you need. Remember the principle of marginal gains – a number of small positive changes are likely to be more effective than one big change.

## A mindful approach to relaxation

The 7:11 and fist-clenching methods described above are generally quick and easy to learn for everyone and are a valuable resource for rescuing yourself from a flare-up or escalating thoughts and catastrophising imaginations. They can be viewed as a tool in the kit-bag to help when needed, a 'go-to' when you need to bring down the body's stress arousal quickly. We teach them for this reason.

Another method is the practice of mindfulness. There are many similarities to 7:11 breathing, but mindfulness methods take longer to learn and some people find them quite challenging. Ultimately, it's best to try different methods with an open mind and discover what works for you in different situations.

Mindfulness meditation is a relaxation approach that gently focuses the attention on moment by moment experience: for example, on the *breath* entering and leaving the nostrils, or on each *part of the body* in turn, or on *sounds* as they occur in our surroundings. Training our attention to focus in this way, accepting what we are experiencing without trying to change anything or make judgments, brings us fully into the present moment, away from worries about the past or unhelpful speculation about the future. This is the essence of cognitive-mindfulness-based stress reduction, an approach that is currently very popular. There is some research evidence emerging that when practised regularly these methods are helping with the management of anxiety disorders, depression and persistent pain.

Choosing where and how we pay attention is the first step to training the mind to be more present and less 'scattered'. Try any of the mindfulness activities below, for five minutes at first, then slowly build up the time you spend. You will notice that the mind tends to skip about all over the place, from thought to thought, and away from the present into the past and future. Each time you realise your attention has gone off track, bring it back to your mindful activity. Be patient with yourself.

The mindful approach can be applied to any activity. Many report how helpful it is while taking exercise, or eating. When applied to eating and drinking it can form part of a weight-management programme. One of the benefits of activities like yoga, tai chi and Pilates, among others, is that they utilise the principles of mindfulness (without necessarily calling it that).

Here are some examples of mindfulness meditations you might like to try.

## Mindful breathing

Sitting or lying down place one hand on the belly or navel area. Notice how the belly rises with the in-breath and drops back with the out-breath. Focus on these physical sensations, with, and then without, the hand in place. There is no emphasis here on trying to change the breath in any way; just allow it to come and go. Rest in the awareness of the physical sensations of the breath moving in and out of the body.

## Mindful standing

Stand with your feet parallel and hip-width apart with the weight equally resting on each foot and allow the knees to soften slightly. Let the arms hang naturally at your sides. Focus attention on finding and maintaining the point where the body is neither over-alert (standing 'to attention') nor over-relaxed (slumping), neither too far forward (with weight balanced through the toes), nor too far back (with weight through the heels). It is often helpful to do this exercise with bare feet or in socks so that sensations from the ground contact points can be focused on.

## Mindful walking

This can be done indoors or outdoors. Find the position of mindful standing described above then focus on a 'pathway' of about ten steps ahead. Start walking very slowly, feeling the feet making contact with the ground. Focus your whole attention on every tiny movement as the heel rises, the calf muscles engage and the foot gradually leaves the ground and is placed down ahead of you. Be aware of how the balance of the body shifts, and how the back foot starts to lift from the heel to make the next step. When you complete your ten steps, turn around slowly and take ten mindful steps back to your starting point.

## Mindful listening

Sit comfortably and bring your attention to your ears. Be aware of any sounds as they arise, wherever they arise, but without searching for them. Allow your awareness to open to sounds both near and far away, in front, behind and inside you, obvious sounds and more subtle sounds, the spaces of silence between sounds.

## Mindful body scan

Make yourself comfortable and take your attention to your left foot. Focus attention on the sensations in your toes. If your attention wanders, as soon as you notice gently bring it back. Gradually focus on each part of the foot in turn, then the lower leg and the upper leg, before taking your focus to your right foot and repeating up the right side. Progress to all areas of the body step by step. You may need to bring your focus back many times – you may even fall asleep. It doesn't matter.

# Practise the art of visualisation

One of the most powerful mental resources we have is our imagination. We can use it to good effect, as when we imagine positive, fulfilling outcomes, or to bad effect, for example when we imagine all kinds of future catastrophes and thus fuel our anxiety. There is a principle called 'The Law of Attraction', first described by William Atkinson in 1906, which states that what you focus on is what you get, and there's a lot of truth in this.

Positive visualisation is a wonderful tool. It enables us to use our imaginations to effect all kinds of changes in our state of mind and how we respond to situations we find ourselves in. We can use it to work towards a goal by visualising the process for achieving success; for example, visualising exercising to improve the level of fitness needed for a walk in the country; or visualising the body's healing system repairing bones or joints; or the brain's ability to turn down the pain volume; or the immune system seeking out and destroying cancer cells. We can also use it to create mental pictures of how our lives will look when we achieve a goal as if it had already occurred; for example, visualising what we will look like and how we will be able to move and what we will be doing when we have returned to good health.

The art of visualisation is used by many successful people, even if they do not use this exact terminology. Sportspeople and those in the performing arts practise success through mental imagery (as well as training the body). Business people develop a clear vision of how they want their business to develop, thereby attuning their consciousness to notice opportunities, products, people and other resources that will support that vision.

The art of visualisation is to use all of your senses, not just 'seeing' but also hearing, smelling, tasting and feeling textures, movements and sensations. We all have a dominant sense, but it is helpful to practise using the full range so that your visualisation becomes an ever-richer experience. Visualisation focuses the attention inwards, creating a deeply relaxed, trance-like state. Trance is a natural condition which we all dip into when we daydream, meditate, jog or otherwise become absorbed in our inner thoughts and experiences. It is sometimes called the REM (rapid eye movement) or 'programming state' and it also occurs when we dream at night. When we access REM, we create powerful images and we are open to new learning. We can do visualisations by ourselves with practice. When it is led by a coach or therapist it is called guided imagery or hypnotherapy. The advertising industry utilises guided imagery all the time to promote a desire for a product or service, thus encouraging us to buy.

## A staircase to relaxation

The following relaxation, from a CD entitled *The therapeutic power of guided imagery,* is a means of taking the relaxation exercises described above to a much deeper level and can be very helpful when you are learning visualisation techniques. (See page 194 for information on where to buy this and other helpful relaxation CDs.)

Make yourself comfortable in a place where you will not be disturbed. Notice how the body is supported – behind the head and back, under the legs and feet. Close your eyes gently. As you breathe in and out, spend a few moments focusing on the belly rising and falling as the breath enters and leaves, without changing or forcing the breath in any way.

Now imagine that you are standing at the top of a flight of ten steps leading down to a special place of relaxation. This could be a place you remember where you felt really calm and peaceful, perhaps a holiday beach, country scene, cosy room, a beautiful garden – or it could be somewhere you invent, the most relaxing place you can possibly imagine.

As your breathing begins to slow down, on each out-breath imagine taking one step down your staircase, holding onto a handrail if you need to. As you slowly descend, count down on each out-breath from 10 to 1, looking forward to the scene that awaits you at the bottom. With your final step, imagine walking into your relaxing space.

Use all your senses to create as vivid a place as possible. See the colours, shapes and quality of light. Hear any sounds that add to your sense of relaxation. There may be smells or even tastes that remind you of calm. You may be able to sense textures under your feet or in your hands; for example, the feeling of soft sand beneath your feet, or the warm, silky water of a bath lapping around your body.

Find somewhere to rest in this scene, as you continue to add more enjoyable features. Begin to notice the sense of relaxation spreading throughout your body, perhaps starting with your feet and working upwards to your head. Notice how your mind has quietened.

When you are ready, imagine leaving your scene, knowing that you can return whenever you wish. Count up from 1 to 10 as you imagine drifting up the staircase, step by step, and walking back into the room. Open your eyes and have a gentle stretch.

Your imagination is your 'reality simulator' so learn to use it wisely. Make sure your attention is focused on what you want more of in your life, the resources that will help you meet important needs. *Remember: what you focus on is what you get.*

## Create a vision of what you want

Try this exercise to help you create a vision of your goals on the pathway to recovery from pain-related disability. Use it frequently during the step-by-step journey towards achieving your goals, and modify it as you progress.

Set aside some quiet time when you won't be interrupted. Close your eyes. Use one of the relaxation techniques described above. The most effective for deep relaxation is the 'Staircase to relaxation'. Once you feel calm and relaxed, gently bring your focus to the future and to the goal you want to achieve.

Let's say, for example, that you want to be able to go dancing with your friends, something you haven't been able to do since your back pain took hold. Imagine you are looking at a cinema screen and a film is playing with you in it, and you are dancing. How do you want to look? Where will it be set? What do you want it to sound or feel like? Put in place the important parts of this vision: the place, the people, how the people (including you) are acting, how you are moving, what music is playing (make it one of your favourites). What is the expression on your face? What do you say when the dance is finished? Make it as vivid as possible, adding detail as it comes to mind. Get a sense of how good it feels to have achieved your vision.

From this place in the future, ask yourself: 'What was the first step I took to achieve my vision? What was the next step, and the next?' Imagine how you have moved, step by step, towards where you want to be in your visualisation. Spend as much time as you wish in this scene. When you are ready, gently count from 1 to 10 to re-orientate yourself back into the room again.

## In summary

- It is crucial to make and protect time for active relaxation in your daily life.
- Learning and practising a means of inducing your biological relaxation response will have important healing effects on your back pain.
- If sleep is a problem, make changes that will improve your sleep hygiene.
- Learning and practising the skill of using imagery to visualise your goals is a powerful tool.

# CHAPTER 10

# MANAGING THOSE DIFFICULT DAYS

S udden episodes of disabling back pain are highly distressing. You are engaged in an activity you have done
a hundred times before, when suddenly you experience
the onset of excruciating pain. It feels overwhelming and
literally knocks you off your feet, leaving you desperate for
anything to relieve the agony. You may end up in an Accident
and Emergency department or need to have a home visit from
a doctor as the pain completely engulfs you, making it impossible for you even to contemplate moving. You might find
yourself stuck in your car seat unable to get up, or stuck in a
restaurant chair unable to move. It's a terrifying and distressing experience.

Even when you have recovered from a difficult day, these
moments sap your confidence in your back and you become
instinctively protective, avoiding excessive movement for fear
of causing a further flare-up. Perplexingly, these difficult days
seem to happen for no reason. You limit activity to try and
protect yourself but this does not seem to reduce the frequency
of flare-ups in back pain. A cycle of uncertainty and unpre-
dictability develops that becomes more and more troublesome
as time goes on. Planning occupational, social or recreational
activities becomes increasingly difficult. And, not surprisingly,
all of this additional distress winds up the pain intensity.

Unfortunately, modern medicine has not found a way to
prevent these difficult days. However, the biopsychosocial

approach focuses on helping people to recognise triggers that can contribute towards bad days, and to have a plan in place to reduce the impact, allowing you to recover quickly and get back on track. This chapter will show you how to get better at managing what we will refer to as 'flare-ups', and to reduce the frequency of such distressing events.

*Managing something involves taking back control, as far as is reasonably possible. And it's easier than you might think.*

## Are there specific triggers for your flare-ups?

Triggers are situations or circumstances that seem to set off a flare-up of your pain. Pain flare-ups can develop gradually, as if a dial on the pain monitor is gradually being turned up, and they can also occur very quickly indeed, as if some switch has suddenly been flicked on.

It is common to believe that all flare-ups in pain are triggered by physical events. Think of the car mechanic who lifts a heavy engine, or the carpenter who lifts a cumbersome shelf unit and experiences a sudden episode of disabling back pain that takes weeks to recover from. These are typical examples of how we used to understand flare-ups in back pain; we thought they were always the result of someone lifting ridiculously heavy weights, ignoring the possible consequences. But we see many people in our clinics who experience flare-ups in back pain while doing very minimal, everyday things such as twisting to pick up a pen from their desk. Many people experience flare-ups in back pain when they haven't moved at all. How can we explain this?

We now recognise that the triggers for flare-ups can be a number of different factors, including physical movements and positions, thoughts and feelings, and the environment itself.

Thoughts and feelings are brain impulses that can trigger physical symptoms, including flare-ups of back pain. Think of the reverse scenario first: recall your favourite song or piece of music and play it in your head for a few moments, really getting absorbed in it. How does it make your body feel? It should promote a release of tension from the muscles. So it's easy to see that the opposite is also true and some thoughts and feelings can make us tense up.

Understanding how these factors contribute to flare-ups is very helpful in allowing you to gain better control over those difficult days and reduce the number of flare-ups you experience.

If you already know that your flare-ups are triggered by your tendency to overdo things, the solution is in your hands. There's advice for those who push themselves too hard on page 155.

Other people notice that their difficult days are triggered by stressful life events, such as an argument with their boss, or dealing with a difficult customer on the phone at work. These types of trigger activate our fight-flight-freeze response and wind up the nervous system, increasing muscle tension. Paradoxically, feeling angry about something and expressing it, 'getting it out of your system', does not seem to trigger a flare-up so often. It is much more likely we will have a flare-up if something upsets us and we do *not* express our feelings about it, as the strong feelings are suppressed. Everyone will face stressful and upsetting situations from time to time but the way we deal with them can make a difference between them causing a flare-up or not. See page 156 for advice on what to do if someone habitually makes you feel bad.

Sometimes people notice that their flare-ups happen in a particular location. This can be the place where they first experienced an episode of distressing back pain. Remember the brain has an extensive filing cabinet where it stores memories of unpleasant and distressing events (as well as pleasurable events and places). This part of the brain recognises patterns – from the environment, all the senses of touch, sight, smell, hearing, temperature, body position, and so on. Without you even being aware of it, at a subconscious level the brain will turn on your fight-flight-freeze response automatically if a threatening situation is perceived. This is because the part of the brain responsible for danger-alert signals is always poised to protect you from danger. It's trying to let you know that 'something out there' is threatening you. This part of the brain lacks precision; it's all instinct. The 'threat' could be a poisonous snake in the long grass of the savannah or it could be the sniping criticism of another person that is undermining your status and integrity. It's a highly sophisticated automatic system that has taken millions of years to evolve and developed long before the higher brain that gives us the ability to think and rationalise. In an emergency, survival instinct always prevails because the thinking brain processes information too slowly and that delay in milliseconds might be the difference between life or death.

For some people their flare-ups are seemingly random events, not influenced by any particular factor they can identify. It's not always a direct chicken-and-egg response but the exercise below might help you to discover a pattern. Sometimes the trigger for a flare-up just pops into mind and surprises you, like a lightbulb switched on in the dark. This only happens when you are sufficiently relaxed to allow the brain to process information. If nothing comes to mind then simply accept the situation for now; over-thinking will make you feel more stressed and the key you are looking for will remain hidden. Be patient with yourself. Perhaps the trigger will become obvious to you on another day.

## Identify your triggers

Make sure you are relaxed and have an open frame of mind. Do one of the relaxation exercises on pages 137–40 if necessary. This lowers your brain's arousal system and allows reflection and learning to take place. Spend a few minutes reflecting on a recent flare-up.

- During the day or so before the flare-up started had you encountered any situation or person that threatened you in any way?
- During the day or so before the flare-up started had you encountered a situation that you found difficult? Did you feel you did not have the resources to deal with it or that you handled the situation badly?
- Had you been anywhere that reminded you of a previous occasion when you were in distress with pain?
- Have you been pushing yourself too hard recently and overdoing it?

## Why do you push yourself so hard?

If your life is frantically busy and there are so many things to manage in your day that you just don't know where to start, you will be increasing your risk of regular flare-ups of back pain. Continually over-activating hypersensitive nerves and muscles, by pushing yourself too hard on a daily basis, will maintain a high level of muscle tension. It then only takes one small extra activity, such as getting out of the car or reaching up to a high cupboard, to tip you into a huge flare-up of pain. You then struggle to work out why doing something you have done hundreds of times before has produced such a huge increase in back pain. It doesn't seem to make sense and is deeply frustrating. Once you have recovered, though, you start to push yourself too hard again, and you get a further episode, this time doing something completely different, such as lifting your shopping onto the kitchen table. But the underlying problem isn't due to the specific activity; it is more to do with pushing yourself too hard in the first place, thus over-activating hypersensitive nerves and muscles.

The underlying reasons why people habitually push themselves too hard are complex. Common themes we have identified in our practice, and which are identified by psychological and behavioural scientists, include:

- Perception of threat: I won't get paid if I don't get this job done on time.
- Perception of threat: my boss will get rid of me if I don't do this properly.
- Perception of threat: people will think badly of me if I show any signs of weakness or ask for help.
- Perception of threat: I will think badly of myself if I show any signs of weakness or ask for help.
- Overcompensating: overdoing an activity we have some control over to compensate for another important area of our life in which we feel inadequate in some way and have little perception of control.

If habitually pushing yourself too hard is adversely affecting your health, aim to make some changes to the likely drivers. Get help to identify them, from a counsellor if need be, and take the necessary action. Start to factor in plenty of recuperation time in your day, as explained in chapter 9, and think about how you can get your emotional needs met without driving yourself so hard (see also chapter 12).

## People who habitually make you feel bad

Some people with back pain who we see in our clinical practice come to recognise that there are certain people in their life who make them feel uncomfortable – perhaps their boss, a work colleague, a partner, relative or friend. They realise that when they are with that person, or even think of being with them, they get tense and anxious. As they grow to understand their back pain better, they make the connection. They notice that sometimes they experience a bad flare-up of their pain when they have recently been in a difficult meeting or social situation, or have had to cope with a difficult phone call with someone who undermines them. Some experience a big flare-up of pain before they even meet the person in question: the anticipation of the encounter acts as a trigger.

If this is happening in your life, then at a biological level, through pattern-matching, the brain is activating the fight-flight-freeze response and will be winding up your pain because of the perceived threat. Your nervous system sensitivity is being ramped up to access more information from the senses and your muscles are being tensed ready for action. The symptoms can develop slowly or very quickly. The effects may last a few hours or for as long as several weeks. If you are spending a lot of time with the person in question, the nervous system never has the chance to rest, and is in a constant state of readiness for action. This will be very tiring for your nervous system. Something will have to give sooner or later. Most likely it will be your health as you break down with an incapacitating episode of pain.

If this is happening to you, then you have three choices:

- You can ignore the warning signs and persevere and accept the pain and suffering the conflict is causing you. Eventually you will break down under the stress and it will then be very difficult to do anything constructive. The repair work required for your emotional health might take a long time.
- You can change the way you react to the conflict and learn to be more assertive. Get some help to do this if needed. Make it one of the goals in your recovery plan.
- You can remove yourself from the environment that is causing the trigger. This might be necessary if all else fails. It might, of course, involve you looking for another job or leaving a relationship that has irretrievably broken down.

Always remember that you cannot aim to change the other person's behaviour or just sit back and hope and pray they will eventually change: this won't happen. All you can do is change the way you respond to their behaviour and/or remove yourself from their environment.

## Taking back control

John was a man who was regularly overwhelmed with flare-ups of back pain that stopped him in his tracks. He could never work out why he was experiencing so many troublesome episodes and could not identify why they were happening. When John learned about the fight-flight-freeze response and how it was linked to his pain, as well as the biological function of pain, he started to shift his attention to identifying situations in which he felt threatened. This was a major change because up to that time he had been trying to notice what might be wrong with his posture, or his chair, or his car seat, or his muscle strength, or worrying about the state of his intervertebral discs. John had recently gone through some personnel changes at work and had a new boss who was consistently undermining him and overloading him with increasing amounts of work. He recognised that when he had a difficult day at work, in which he had been criticised by his boss, he felt more tense, and noticed this could trigger significant episodes of low back pain. He discovered he was usually distressed before a flare-up and recognised that his relationship with his boss was a key trigger to this distress and the resulting flare-ups in back pain. John normally wore a suit to work and he even noticed, on reflection, that his back pain frequently reduced in intensity as soon as he slipped his jacket off on arriving home. He had been completely unaware of this before gaining this new and empowering understanding.

John began to talk about the pressure he felt under at work in a way he had never done before. He usually ignored his feelings, kept his head down and soldiered on: this was his style. Now he decided to be more assertive in order to protect himself and his needs. However, his anxiety levels were running quite high even when he was just thinking about his work situation. Following a little coaching, John used the 7:11 breathing technique (see page 137) to calm himself down so that he could think clearly and act more effectively. He started to respond to his boss's requests that he take on more and more work by asking which tasks could be given a lower priority to make the necessary time for the latest high-priority job.

John started to feel in more control of these encounters. His pain eased off and he no longer experienced any flare-ups, although he learned to recognise that if his pain was becoming more bothersome it could be because something in his life was getting out of balance and needed attention. He began to discuss his feelings about the things that cause him anxiety with his wife. He became more relaxed at home, he slept better and his relationships within the family improved. Soon he became aware that his boss was backing off somewhat and not being so demanding. Once he changed his response, John discovered that his boss's bullying behaviour towards him was changing.

Reflecting on his experience, John said the lightbulb moment was when he understood his pain as the brain's response to threat rather than something structurally wrong in his spine. That was the key to him finding and dealing with the cause of his pain.

## Feeling over-stressed

Every single one of us needs a certain amount of stress in order to get things done, to stretch us to learn new skills, and to do our jobs well. You just don't want too much of it. Ongoing, unresolved chronic stress damages health in many different ways and is a common trigger for the first distressing episode of back pain or for subsequent flare-ups.

Stress, of course, is our body's biological response to a perceived threat. It is remarkably common for us to learn that in the period leading up to the first significant episode of back pain or before a significant worsening of pain, the person had been experiencing stress-related symptoms of one kind or another as a result of difficult life events or circumstances. They tried to keep going through these circumstances. The warning signs were there but were ignored or not recognised, and coping strategies were near breaking point. There comes a point when the brain, out to protect us as always, has to respond by putting the brakes on in an overwhelming freeze (emergency) response that locks us up so drastically that we cannot move or do anything.

By now you will have learned some steps you can take to unlock this vicious cycle of stress/flare-ups. Later in this chapter we will show you how to create a flare-up action plan.

## Flare-ups caused by the environment

Some people tell us that their flare-ups happen in particular places. This may sound strange, but if we return to what we know about persistent pain and structural changes in the brain, it becomes easier to understand.

There is an area in your brain that asks the questions 'Have I been here before? Is it familiar?' It stores all your memories from past experiences, then when you experience something new, it checks this new experience against what has happened before. If, in your past, you have experienced a distressing episode of back pain in a certain location, your brain will remember the pattern. When you return to that location, or somewhere remarkably similar, the guard-room part of the brain (known as the amygdala) will instantaneously detect this pattern match as a threatening situation and will prepare you for action, raising your nerve-muscle tension and activating the fight-flight-freeze response. This will all happen subconsciously, in an instant, without you 'knowing' it. You may experience a flare-up there and then, or you may experience it later in the day, as the nerve-muscle tension builds up.

Learning to recognise what is happening, and why, is important, so that you can apply your flare-up action plan.

---

### Yasmeen's bad day

Yasmeen was a nurse who had been troubled by persisting back pain for at least a year. Her pain was preventing her from enjoying many activities, including work, and it had really been getting her down. She had been signed off work for the last three months and felt no better for it, and she missed her job. She was keen to improve her ability to walk longer distances, which she hadn't been able to do for many months.

Yasmeen attended one of our rehabilitation programmes and made great progress over a period of a few weeks. She started a phased return to work and was using a graded walking programme to increase the time she could spend walking. She was starting to feel as if she was getting her life back again. On the last day of the programme, she was in the changing rooms of the physiotherapy gym getting ready for her final exercise session. She reached to put her coat on a peg and developed a sudden flare-up of her back pain. She came into the session distressed and in tears, annoyed and frustrated by what had happened, desperate to get on with her final exercise session but finding it difficult to move. She worried that all the good work she had done over the previous few weeks had been fruitless and felt worried about whether she would ever get over this setback. Her negative catastrophising thoughts were racing. Yasmeen felt stiff and stuck, both physically and psychologically. She couldn't work out why she was

---

experiencing such a bad episode of pain after simply reaching up to put her coat on a peg, something she had done several times before without any problem. It just didn't make sense.

We helped Yasmeen do a body scan to check the symptoms she was feeling were familiar; they were. It was definitely a flare-up. Taking her aside we invited her to lie down on her back on a mat and to focus all of her attention on 7:11 breathing. Yasmeen did this for about 10 minutes and was visibly more relaxed afterwards.

Once she had relaxed she was able to talk through what she had been doing that morning. She told us she had taken her dog for the usual walk. Anything different? Well yes, after a long spell of dry weather in the autumn, it had rained over night. There were many slippery wet leaves about. We asked Yasmeen to re-wind her memory to the very first distressing episode of back pain she had experienced and tell us about it. She told us that it had been the previous autumn. She was out walking her dog on a wet morning when there were lots of dead leaves on the ground. She slipped on the pavement, fell, and landed really awkwardly in the road, with her dog pulling at her on its lead. In an instant she saw a car coming towards her. The car skidded as the driver hit the brakes and luckily it did not hit her. Yasmeen needed help from passers-by to get her up and back home, and her back was very painful later that day. She had it checked in the Accident and Emergency department of her local hospital and no serious injury or broken bone was detected so she was sent home with a diagnosis of 'common back strain'.

This had been a very traumatic and potentially life-threatening experience for Yasmeen, and her brain remembered every detail of the circumstances. She had been out with her dog on the same walk many times since this accident, despite her back pain, but had never experienced a flare-up like this one. However, on this particular morning, the environment was an exact pattern match: wet leaves, autumn, time of day, shiny pavement, dog on the lead, cars passing … Her brain computed there was a threat, that her life might be in danger. The result of this was that her fight-flight-freeze response had been turned right up that morning, raising her nerve-muscle tension. It then only took one small trigger – twisting slightly to hang up her coat – to initiate a large pain output and the flare-up happened.

Talking this through, it all made sense to Yasmeen. She stopped worrying that she had damaged her back and her racing negative thoughts stopped. She was able to recover from the flare-up within 20 minutes and immediately joined in with some physical exercise. She successfully returned to work and some months later was doing well and felt in no need of further help.

## Creating a flare-up action plan

Flare-ups of back pain are to be expected so it is best to be prepared for them. In this section we'll explain how to have an action plan or, if you prefer, a set of tools in your toolkit that you know how to use when needed.

*The first step is to identify then stop any catastrophising thoughts. The way you respond to a flare-up is the most important factor that influences the outcome.*

When flare-ups happen, our capacity for rational thinking gets taken over. The stronger the pain, the more this occurs. Because pain demands attention and always has an emotional component, the survival part of our brain dominates events. The stronger the emotional response – fear, catastrophising thoughts and over-active imaginations – the more the rational, thinking part of the brain is hijacked. The longer this goes on, the stronger the pain and the longer it takes to get over it. Negative thoughts and feelings invade you and make you feel as if your whole life is out of control, as figure 17 illustrates.

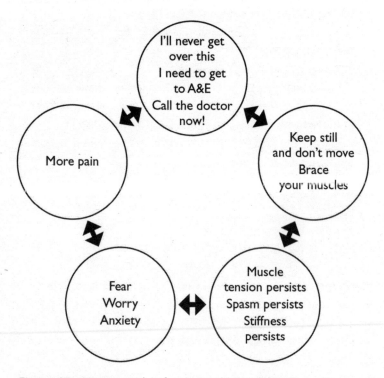

Figure 17 - Vicious cycle of catastrophising following a flare-up.

Having a plan to arrest catastrophising thoughts when you get a flare-up and reframe them, as shown in figure 18, will dramatically speed up your recovery.

You *can* choose to react differently. By changing how you *think* when you experience a flare-up, you will discover that you *do* things differently. You will feel more confident that you can recover quickly. You will find it is easier to get moving sooner, safe in the knowledge that you haven't caused any damage to your back. You will be in more control. This will

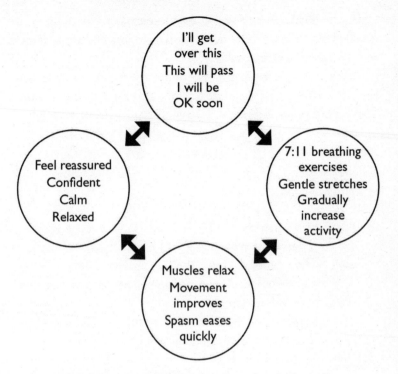

Figure 18 – Reframing catastrophic thoughts during a flare-up.

reduce your anxiety, which will reduce the pain and release tension in the muscles.

| Catastrophic thoughts | Reassuring thoughts |
| --- | --- |
| I'll never get over this | This will pass eventually |
| Something awful is happening inside my back | It's not damaged; I will recover soon |
| Oh no, this is terrible. What have I done? | I've been here before; it will get better soon |
| My back feels as if it is lopsided | I just need to calm my muscles down |

If you check your thoughts when you have a flare-up, you will be able to make real meaningful changes, and allow yourself to recover much quicker.

But it doesn't stop there. There are many other things you can do when you have a flare-up that will limit its impact and help you to recover quickly. It is good to have your own flare-up plan to help your recovery, but the list below is a good starting point.

## A plan for flare-ups

- *Keep calm.* As soon as possible relax yourself using one of the exercises described in chapter 9. 7:11 breathing is particularly useful in this sort of situation. This is when you need it!
- *Accept it has happened.* This doesn't mean giving in to it; it's just accepting it. This mindset lowers the stress levels quickly and facilitates recovery. The alternative is to set up a battle with the pain, to get cross or try to ignore it: these are all guaranteed to raise stress levels and make you suffer more and for longer.
- *Do a quick body scan to make sure that the flare-up is familiar.* Check that it is in the same region of your body, and that it is similar to previous flare-ups. If it is, it's highly likely that there is no new damage and you can start a recovery plan immediately. If your pain is unfamiliar, if it is spreading to a different body region, or if you feel unwell or have a temperature associated with it, you should get it checked out by a health professional. Revisit the Red Flags box on page 16 to help you decide whether you need medical advice.
- *Check your thoughts to make sure you are not catastrophising.* Reassure yourself that the pain will pass soon.
- *Do some 7:11 breathing exercises.* Repeat frequently. This will activate your body's natural relaxation response and will soon help to calm down cramping, sensitive muscles and speed up recovery.
- *When you feel ready, do some gentle exercises.* Try some of the stretches from chapter 8, or any of your own stretches that

have helped in the past. It pays to have practised these before so you are familiar with them. It's no good trying something new in an emergency. Always do some 7:11 breathing before you start stretching. Muscles are likely to move better if they are in a relaxed state. Remember to breathe out as you go into each stretch.

- *Modify your activity.* If you have made plans for the day, decide what you can skip or delegate to other people. Let someone you trust know you are having a bad day and ask for help if needed. Maintain physical activity, although you may have to modify it for a short while, and make time for short spells of active relaxation.

- *Reframe how you view your flare-up.* Recognise that the sudden increase in pain and muscle spasm is most likely due to your fight-flight-freeze system working overtime, rather than actual injury to your back. Learn to see these difficult spells as an opportunity to discover new ways of getting on top of your back pain, trying out new strategies, and spotting the triggers.

- *Use medication if you need to.* Short-term use of medication can be helpful as part of flare-up management as it can ease the pain and allow you to get moving. You are more likely to recover quickly if you combine medication with some of the other strategies listed here. Do not rely on medication alone.

- *Return to normal activities as soon as possible.* While it is helpful to accept that normal activity needs to be modified initially, getting moving will speed your recovery. It is better not to wait until your back pain has settled before you return to normal activities, but to see this as part of your recovery plan.

- *Reward yourself for managing it well.* When you do something that directly helps you recover with less down-time, remember to reward yourself. Give yourself a pat on the back as a minimum. It is easy to forget this bit. Many people are too hard on themselves. Children learn best by rewarding positive behaviour and adults are the same.

- *Reflect on and learn from the experience.* What did you do that worked? Why did it work? What didn't work so well? What trigger(s) are you able to identify that will help you understand your pain better? Can you do something about the trigger to reduce the chance of relapse? Remember that triggers commonly include physical ones, such as excessive tiredness, as well as emotional and environmental factors, and they will always be unique to you. No two people will have the same triggers.

## In summary

- Flare-ups will happen sometimes.
- Accepting the situation rather than getting cross and setting up a battle with it will give you a much better chance of early recovery with less or no down-time.
- You must stop catastrophising thoughts and an over-active imagination immediately.
- Learn and practise a plan for a flare-up so it is ready as a toolkit when you need it.
- If you remember nothing else, do the 7:11 breathing exercises. These alone will help get you out of trouble.
- Aim to accept the flare-up as an opportunity to learn more about your pain response and what might be triggering it.
- Reward yourself for success and don't beat yourself up if the strategy did not work so well: try something different next time.

# CHAPTER 11

# GETTING THE MOST OUT OF WORK

Persistent back pain impacts greatly on our ability to work. And by work we mean any meaningful activity: whether paid employment, voluntary work, care-giving or nurturing. Back pain remains one of the commonest reasons for sickness absence from employment worldwide. Some have to take the odd day off every now and then, while others take a prolonged period of sick leave, particularly when they have had a severe episode of back pain. It is difficult to return to work again if you still have persistent back pain, but in this chapter we have some advice on how to manage. If you have a job to return to, we call this 'occupational rehabilitation'.

Sadly, some are never able to return to work; they lose their jobs and have to rely on support of one form or another. This makes it even more difficult to re-engage with the world of work. These people need help with 'vocational rehabilitation'.

Before we look at this in more detail it is important to acknowledge that work is generally good for you. We may not think this on a wet, dark, grey Monday morning in a cold warehouse, or towards the end of a long busy day of meetings, emails and phone calls, but there is overwhelming evidence from many studies that work is generally good for health and wellbeing. Whatever measure of health status is used, it is better when the individual is in work. Only one qualification needs to be made when we say work is good for our health: it needs to be *satisfying work*.

Work gives us all an identity, a sense of purpose in life and a reason to get out of bed in the morning. Without regular work, many people feel they have no direction, and can then develop other health problems, both physically and mentally. Being out of work, whether paid employment or care-giving, is linked to a much greater risk of common health problems.

People with back pain face many obstacles to returning to work or staying in work. Here are some possible ones:

- You are advised to stay off work for extended periods of time. This is unhelpful and will delay recovery.
- Your manager doesn't support and encourage a return to work, saying 'Don't return until you are 100% better'. Returning to work, initially on reduced hours or in a modified role, will usually speed up your recovery, while staying off can delay recovery.
- You are waiting for tests or specialist appointments; sometimes people are told by medical professionals to stay off work until they have their 'results'. This can often take weeks, and means you are waiting around unnecessarily. This will delay your return to work and delay your recovery.
- Uncertainty: when you have back pain, it can be difficult to know what to do for the best. Employers sometimes feel like this too. But getting moving at reduced levels initially then gradually increasing your workload is nearly always the best way to go.
- Lack of opportunity for modified duties; some workplaces are unable to offer part-time contracts or fewer duties. If this is the case, then doing your normal job but with reduced hours initially helps.

| Myths about work and back pain | The reality |
|---|---|
| Back pain is made worse by working | While work may be uncomfortable or difficult for a time, it rarely causes any lasting damage |

| | |
|---|---|
| Having back pain means you have underlying damage or disease | In most instances this is not the case. There is often little or no underlying damage or disease. Even when there is, long-term absence from work is not inevitable |
| Back pain should be treated with rest | Activity is usually best. Much modern treatment encourages and supports continuing or returning to ordinary activities, including work, as soon as possible |
| Having back pain means you need to be signed off sick for several weeks | Often this is not helpful. Most workers manage to remain at work or return to work fairly quickly, even though symptoms may persist or recur. Long-term absence from work is rarely necessary or helpful |
| You need to stay off work until your pain has gone | This is usually unnecessary, unrealistic, and unhelpful. Work is therapeutic and return to work is an essential part of rehabilitation. Your employer should help you to return as early as possible, even while some symptoms remain |
| Having back pain means you need permanently modified work | This can actually be harmful. Work or workplace adjustments should only be temporary in periods of flare-up |
| Back pain will be cured by medical treatment | Healthcare is usually not the whole answer. Treatment may help the symptoms, but usually does not 'cure' back pain forever |

Adapted from Work and Health leaflet (2006) by Waddell and Burton

## Managing the return to work

Having a graded approach to returning to work, either by going back to your normal role on reduced hours, or returning to work in a modified role, will help you gradually to restore function and confidence in your back and your work. The longer

you leave returning to work, the harder it is to return successfully. Those changes in the nervous and musculoskeletal systems
we described in chapters 3 and 4 will become more established
the longer you delay a return to normal activities, and over time
returning to work will seem more and more difficult, which will
of course wind up the nervous system and maintain pain.

To help you understand how you can best help yourself, let's
look at three different scenarios regarding work and back pain.

- You are at work, but struggling due to your back pain.
- You are off work, but still have a job to get back to.
- You have not worked for six months or more and are planning
  to return to some form of work.

> ☛ 'I'm at work but struggling. I need to take days off
>   now and then and I'm worried about being able
>   to remain in my current role.'

If you can relate to this experience, many of the principles we
have introduced you to in previous chapters will help. If you
suffer from repeated flare-ups in back pain, for example, applying the principles in the flare-up plan will help you to recover
more quickly. Reassuring yourself that it's safe to get moving,
and putting a recovery plan in place as soon as you have a flare-
up, will reduce the impact of the pain, allowing you to maintain
your work responsibilities.

If you are struggling at work, we advise that you discuss
this informally with your manager. It's best to do this before a
crisis occurs, when you may feel you cannot do anything other
than stay off for a prolonged period. Open up an informal
dialogue. Explain that when you are having trouble with your
back, it would be helpful if you could spend a day or two in
a modified role, to allow you to get over your flare-up. Most
employers are happier if their employees are in work doing
something, even if they can't be quite as productive as normal,
than if they are at home in bed.

Many people we see, however, feel uncomfortable discussing this with their manager, because they don't want to be perceived as a 'weak link' in the organisation. It's normal to feel like this, but often informal arrangements with good employers, to help you when you are having a bad day, will limit the impact that flare-ups in back pain can have on both you and the organisation you work for. Remember, it is your employer's duty to support you in a way that will help you stay in work if you have back pain (and other common health problems). Use their support wisely. Be as specific as possible with your requests for help.

If you can't face discussing this with your manager, there may be other people within your organisation who are able to help. Many medium-sized and larger companies will have an occupational health advisor either visiting the site or available for telephone consultations. Occupational health advisors have an ethical duty to advise what is best for *your* health even though your employer pays their salary. Some people nevertheless feel uncomfortable doing this; they think it makes their problem more formal, and worry it could result in them losing their job. Be assured: employment laws dictate that an employer cannot dismiss you for a health problem without having first gone through due process of supporting a return-to-work programme or considering modified or alternative work if available, and also gathering opinions from your GP (with your consent) or an independent medical advisor.

Another person who may be able to help you is your GP. In the UK, your GP is one of the health professionals responsible for assessing your fitness for work. They can make recommendations to your employer, to help you manage your back pain flare-ups at work most effectively. Union representatives can also be of assistance by supporting mediation and facilitating your support at work or your return to work after an absence.

So if you are struggling to remain in your current job due to your back pain, we encourage you to learn and apply the principles in this book as well you are able. Making a number of small changes in your day-to-day life all add up and will be really helpful in your function and comfort. Most people will be able to manage the trouble their back gives them using their own resources. However, for a few this is not enough; if you continue to struggle at work, seek help from your employer. There is a lot at stake.

☞ 'I'm off work but want to find a way to get back.'

If this describes your current predicament, there are several things you can do to make a successful return to work more likely.

Some people tell us that their employer has never contacted them while they were off work. This understandably might make you feel isolated and as if the employer doesn't care. If that is the case, it is essential for your health to set up channels of communication. Taking some control of a return-to-work plan will make you more confident you can achieve it. Contacting your manager, or human resources department, or occupational health advisor will be an important first step.

Approach this with a positive frame of mind and explain what work you currently feel capable of taking on. If you feel unable to take on any aspect of work then explain what help you are seeking to aid your recovery. Ask your employer to support a phased return to your usual job when you are ready and give an estimate of the time you expect this to take. This gives you a degree of control and autonomy and greatly assists your employer. He or she may have hired someone else to do your work while you are absent, so many other people are affected. Open and frequent solution-focused communication is essential to find the best outcome for all concerned.

A phased return to work uses the principles of graded activity we discussed in chapter 6, gradually challenging your body to increase your activity levels progressively. It is current best practice for return to any form of employment after an extended period of time away due to health problems.

It is normal to feel some degree of apprehension about returning to work, particularly if you have been off for several weeks or months. Reassure yourself that unless you start to test your ability now, you will never know whether you can manage it or not. People usually surprise themselves by how much they are able to manage comfortably when they return to work and they feel better for it.

The introduction of the 'fit note' gave GPs in the UK the opportunity to advise your employer that you are able to undertake modified duties or a phased return. But remember that your GP does not know your job the way you do. Have a constructive and open conversation with your GP about what you think would be a good starting point, ensuring that you are leading the conversation. This is a much better way to tackle returning to work than relying on others to make the decisions for you. Doing it this way will help you to feel in control of the return-to-work plan, and make it more likely that you will be successful.

It is important to recognise that the longer you have been off work, the more difficult it will be to return. Many of the biological changes in your body we discussed in chapters 3 and 4 become established after a long period during which you are not doing your normal daily activities, and over time people become more apprehensive and anxious about returning to work. This will turn up and maintain your pain. A feeling of helplessness and hopelessness soon starts to take over.

*Starting on a phased return-to-work plan as soon as possible is best for you, your back, your health, and your future employment prospects.*

You may feel worse for a short period of time as you get going but stay focused on realistic and achievable goals that you agree to and the journey will be easier.

Finally, if there is an aspect of your work that is making you unhappy then do something about it. Once again you have three choices:

- Ignore the warning signs and persevere, hoping the problem will go away or someone else will fix it.

- Change your response to the problem: learn assertiveness skills if the problem is inter-personal, or ask for changes or help if the job isn't right for you. Protect yourself from the stress work is causing you by making time for pleasurable activities in your life and remembering to relax regularly.
- Look for another job.

> ☞ You haven't worked for months, or even years, but want to get back to work

Some people with persistent back pain who have not worked for prolonged periods of time are never able to return to any form of paid employment. There can be a variety of different reasons. However, be assured that this is not the case for most people with back pain.

The information in previous chapters has provided you with a new understanding of your back pain, and introduced the concept of taking back responsibility for your recovery and setting goals. In our society when a person has been out of work for a length of time due to back pain, there are a number of additional obstacles to overcome:

- You will be at a disadvantage in an open job market when applying for waged work.
- You will have lost confidence in your ability to fulfil the responsibilities that are part of any job.
- You will have de-skilled. Perhaps your IT skills are out of date and need to be refreshed.
- You will have lost confidence in your ability to present yourself effectively at a job interview.
- You will have become physically deconditioned.
- You will have lost contacts you previously enjoyed when in the world of work.
- Others within your family will have adapted to having you at home all the time – for better or for worse.

These obstacles are real and can be formidable to overcome at the best of times. You are going to need a lot of determination, and a lot of support from your family, professionals and employment agencies.

A very practical solution that has helped all the people we have known who have successfully made the transition back to work is to use the voluntary sector. Taking on a job as, say, a volunteer driver for a local hospice or charitable institution, volunteering in hospitals or care homes, volunteering for outdoor work such as conservation or wildlife projects – there are many opportunities. When you return to work routines, doing a worthwhile job and interacting with people outside your immediate family, your confidence and fitness will quickly increase. Before long, new opportunities will open up for you.

CHAPTER 12

# MAINTAINING AN IMPROVED QUALITY OF LIFE

Let us recap what has been covered so far:

- Persistent pain comes primarily from the nervous system, and this can be retrained.
- Our thoughts, feelings and habits affect our pain experience.
- Our lifestyles affect our pain experience: physical activity, work, rest and relaxation should all be in balance.

Now it's time, if you have not done so already, to step aside and reflect on the timeline of your pain experience. Many people we work with say this exercise has been the key to liberating themselves from persistent pain as they gain an understanding of the deeper meaning of their experience. You cannot benefit from this exercise if you are tense and anxious or worrying about something. Before starting, do a relaxation exercise such as 7:11 breathing to get you in a calm state of mind.

Start by asking yourself what else was going on in your life at the time of a recent flare-up of your pain or during your first distressing episode of pain?

It's useful to use the analogy of a bathtub to explore this further (see figure 19 below).

Water flows into the bathtub from the tap. Water flows out of the bathtub down the drain. If the level of water is too high in the bathtub, water escapes down the overflow pipe.

Imagine the water level represents the amount of neuro-muscular tension in your body at any one point of time. This is constantly changing but there will always be a certain amount of tension in the body somewhere, most of it outside of our awareness. The musculoskeletal tension hangs around, not surprisingly, in our vulnerable areas, where it can cause back aches, headaches, or any regional pain problem. The tension may affect the digestive or excretion systems, causing irritable bowel syndrome or bladder problems. It may influence the immune system and create relapses of conditions that are closely linked to the functioning of the immune system, such as eczema, psoriasis, allergies and many more.

The brain becomes alarmed when water starts to flow down the overflow: it might be a dribble that starts and stops at intervals or it might be one big rush. When the brain feels

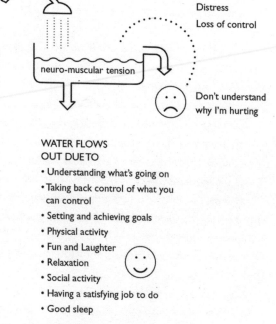

WATER FLOWS
IN DUE TO

• Distressing life events
• Loss of any kind
• Transitions of life
• Trauma/illness
• Conflicts
• A difficult important relationship
• Overstriving
• Sedentary lifestyle
• Poor quality sleep

neuro-muscular tension

Distress
Loss of control

Don't understand
why I'm hurting

WATER FLOWS
OUT DUE TO

• Understanding what's going on
• Taking back control of what you can control
• Setting and achieving goals
• Physical activity
• Fun and Laughter
• Relaxation
• Social activity
• Having a satisfying job to do
• Good sleep

Figure 19 – The bathtub analogy explaining
neuro-muscular tension.

alarmed, the amount of neuro-muscular tension in the body is raised and it is more likely that pain will be experienced.

The tap filling the bathtub runs faster when we are going through difficult life events or anything that distresses us. The list is long and includes loss of loved ones, work or pursuits closely linked to our identity; it can include trauma or transitions in life, such as leaving home, starting a first job, getting married, or undergoing role changes as children leave home, elderly parents have to be cared for, you or your partner retire from work; it can include stress from difficult relationships, holding onto perceived injustice, anger, fear or guilt that has now outlived its usefulness, or unresolved conflicts ... and more. You get the idea.

The tap also runs faster when we are struggling to maintain something unsustainable: many of us try to live up to expectations we set ourselves to please everyone and try to do everything perfectly. We habitually take on more than we can possibly manage, including other people's problems, and ignore our own needs. You get the idea.

Water runs out through the plughole more quickly when we are doing something pleasurable and satisfying, something we are good at; when we get the rest we need; when we stop over-using medications that are not working for us; when we shift our attention away from introspection and dwelling on all the negative aspects of our situation; when we experience fun and laughter, social activities, physical exercise we enjoy, feeling in control of what is within our capacity to control, giving up trying to control things we cannot control. Knowing the difference. You get the idea.

This model helps us understand why flare-ups of pain or the very first significant episode of back pain can occur when we do not seem to have done anything very much to trigger them. The bathtub had very likely been running close to overflowing for some time; maybe the warning signs were there but we ignored or did not recognise them. Then suddenly a massive pain experience, disproportionate to what you would normally expect, struck us. There was too much water flowing in through the tap and not enough water flowing out down the plughole.

So it is helpful to:

- Recognise what is or has been flowing through the tap and turn down or stop what you can control.
- Accept what you cannot change.
- Do what is within your control to speed up the outflow. Understanding what is going on will slow down or stop the flow through the tap.

In doing this, you may be able to identify some of the previously hidden triggers and understand why your back pain fluctuates from day to day, week to week or month to month.

### Mark's bathtub moment

Mark had been struggling with back pain for a number of years, which meant he had difficulty with many aspects of daily living. He joined the functional restoration programme and discovered new ways of understanding his problems. He benefited from the graded approach to exercise especially and achieved his desired goal of returning to play regular games of badminton in his club. He was in the habit of taking short walking and stretch breaks during the working day and came to realise how important this was, especially as his job was sedentary (he was a specialist in computer-aided design in an engineering company) and he travelled to work by car. Things went well for six months or so after the programme.

Then something changed. A new work project meant that Mark needed to travel abroad frequently, and was away two or three days most weeks. He wasn't keen on taking this project but it was an important contract and he didn't want to let the company down. His back started aching again, at first during meetings, then it became more bothersome during other activities as well. His health seemed to be taking a step backwards and he felt depressed. All the progress he had made seemed to

MAINTAINING AN IMPROVED QUALITY OF LIFE

be coming undone. He was annoyed with himself and started to dwell on his back problems, which made him feel worse. He tried blaming the different beds and chairs he was having to use. Then one day, while having a shower in a hotel where you had to stand in a bathtub (he had a walk-in shower at home), he suddenly remembered the bathtub talk we had given and realised it applied to him. At that moment, he resolved to do something about his situation.

When he got home, he sat down with his wife once their children were in bed and they drew a bathtub sketch, like the one on page 180. Together they listed what had been filling his bathtub recently.

*The tap*: change in work routine and additional pressure to make a contract work; taking work home; the novelty of travel had worn off and airports and hotels were becoming a chore. Deep down he felt angry with his boss for asking him to take on this work and with himself for agreeing to do it when deep down he was not happy with it. He had realised previously that he had a tendency to say 'yes' too readily when under pressure and yet he fell into it again. The introspection and blaming chairs and beds was creating yet more stress arousal that was feeding more water into the tap.

*The plughole*: since taking on the new work he had not had time to play badminton and he missed it, both for the exercise it gave him and for the motivation to stay fit. He used to hang around after a game and have a drink and a chat with a good friend but since he wasn't playing this important social contact had dropped off during recent months. The travel had unsettled his routine and he was forgetting to take mini relaxation breaks during the working days.

This all started to make sense and Mark was able to understand why his pain was getting worse as his nervous system was tuning up to alarm state again. Discussing it with his wife and looking at the bathtub sketch helped him to see what he could do to rebalance the water level. He arranged a meeting with his manager and explained that the current workload with all the extra travelling was putting his health at risk and he wanted things to change. He put forward some ideas and the two of them agreed a plan to bring in an additional person to help with the overseas work so that Mark could work from head office more, doing something he was good at. This would allow regular time for recreational activities. Mark returned to the badminton club and decided to get more involved by joining the committee organising social activities in order to widen his network of friends. He also decided to earmark time for active relaxation by joining a yoga-mindfulness class one evening a week: this was a new skill to learn which stretched him in different ways. Both he and his family enjoyed a better quality of life as his back pain settled down again. And he enjoyed his work more as balance was restored to his life.

Plan for this. You will need to get into the habit of monitoring how you are doing, especially when circumstances change. Flare-ups or setbacks will provide the opportunity for reflecting on how your maintenance plan is going. Keep reassessing your goals as you go along. Set new challenges for yourself from time to time: try a new activity, and push for higher levels of fitness when you are able. One goal might be to take time out every day to relax and reflect on how you are reacting to events in your life and to visualise changes you might want to make. With practice, this need only take ten minutes or so out of your day.

## Gavin's story revisited

It was a wet Tuesday morning at the Royal Orthopaedic Hospital. Walking across the car park towards the physiotherapy gym, David Rogers became aware of a person who looked familiar walking towards him. They both stopped. The other person was Gavin.

'You don't remember me, do you?' said Gavin.

David shook Gavin's hand. 'Of course I do.'

David remembered the first time he saw Gavin when he started the functional restoration programme some two years previously. The change in Gavin during those two years had been remarkable. As they spoke Gavin told him that he remembered all the principles he had learned on the programme: about graded activity, 7:11 breathing, withdrawing from the pain medication, gentle and regular stretching, taking rest and relaxation breaks, and taking back control of himself so as to manage flare-ups.

Gavin said that after working on his recovery, he decided not to return to his singing career. It had been too full on and demanding. He looked around at employment opportunities, knowing how important it was for his health and wellbeing to have some fulfilling work to do. He had recently applied for a job in the IT department at the Royal Orthopaedic Hospital, and was offered a position on the help desk. Although this meant Gavin would spend some time sitting at a desk, he would also have to transport IT equipment around the hospital site, preparing and installing new machines. This, of course, involved bending, lifting and twisting and spending several hours at a time on his feet.

Gavin enjoyed this new challenge and since then has provided regular and reliable service and has become a popular figure around the hospital. During this time, he has been pleasantly surprised that he has not had any distressing flare-ups of back pain. He did return to singing on stage several months ago: a one-off special performance for his bride, on their wedding day, in front of his invited family and guests.

Gavin has also found another role, one he would never have dreamed of a few years ago.

He now works on a voluntary basis as our expert patient, helping groups of people with persistent back pain on their journeys towards recovery. Gavin reflects on his own experience of back pain, explaining the traumatic journey he went through when his back pain first presented, his natural scepticism about the merits of using the biopsychosocial approach for his back pain, and how he continues to use what he has learned to maintain all the gains made. This now takes little effort because the ideas and skills of stretching and 7:11 breathing have become habit.

He says it is important to keep an open mind about the ideas and practices taught on the programme and urges people to try things for themselves. This is different from many other approaches to treating back pain – but if you always do the same thing you will keep getting the same results. Yes, it can be hard at times, and there might be times when you doubt you will ever make progress. Gavin admits that it can test your resolve but he says it will ultimately bring out the best in you as you learn to get on top of back pain that has previously defeated you. And he is able to share his own experience: that over the two years since he took part in our programme, not only has he got his life back again, but it is better in many ways than it was before.

## In summary

Persistent back pain continues to blight many people's lives, but combined physical and psychological approaches to treatment, using a biopsychosocial approach as described in this book, offers real potential for recovery of function and improved quality of life. Having a good understanding of what is happening in our bodies when back pain persists is a key first step. Once you understand that persistent back pain often has more to do with changes in the nervous system than any other body structures, you can start to do something about these changes. This will empower you to recover, however much your back pain presently impacts on your daily life.

Acknowledging that we learn to move and even think differently when back pain persists, and finding ways to restore normal movement and activity, safe in the knowledge that persistent back pain is not indicative of tissue damage, will give you confidence that recovery is possible. Using graded activity principles, combining stretching, aerobic exercise and activities linked to your goals, and practising relaxation techniques regularly, will help you to unlock your own personal pathway to recovery. Having a structured plan to tackle those difficult days when flare-ups occur will put you back in control of your life, allowing you to plan confidently for the future. And maintaining these changes will mean that not only will you get back to life, but will stay there in the long run.

We see people get 'Back to Life' every week in clinical practice and we hope that the biopsychosocial approach described in this book will give you confidence that recovery in function and quality of life is within your teach.

# ACKNOWLEDGEMENTS

Between us, we have been treating people with back pain for a combined total of 35 years and it is difficult to acknowledge everyone who has contributed to our evolution as clinicians, whether they are work colleagues, researchers or experts in the field of back pain. However, there are some people who have been key to our development.

Special mention must go to the clinicians who have helped inspire us both during our careers. These include Sharon Wilday, who introduced us to the benefits of using a cognitive behavioural approach to treating patients, and Gail Sowden, a physiotherapist who has been a leading light in promoting combined physical and psychological approaches for helping people with back pain. Other clinicians with whom we have worked closely using the biopsychosocial approach are Nigel Haddock, a physiotherapist, and Abigail Darling, a Human Givens Therapist and pain counsellor who works with us on our functional restoration programmes. We have been supported in our work by several spinal surgeons; special thanks to Mel Grainger, Adrian Gardiner and Alistair Stirling at the Royal Orthopaedic Hospital. Our team of physiotherapists and Extended Scope Physiotherapists within the Centre for Musculoskeletal Medicine at the Royal Orthopaedic Hospital have been key in supporting us to help develop our service, along with our excellent administration support team. Also, having a clinical manager with an open mind, who is prepared to put research into practice and allow a service to evolve and develop, has made a huge difference to our ability to grow an effective service; in this regard, Nicola Mason has been an essential player for us.

On a wider perspective, the contribution of Dr George Engel, who pioneered the idea that psychological and social factors could influence health and was responsible for the birth of the biopsychosocial approach, has influenced much of the work in this area, including our own programme. The work of Gordon Waddell in the late 1990s applied this model to back pain patients, and his book *The Back Pain Revolution* transformed the way we helped people with back pain restore function and quality of life. Ronald Melzack and Patrick Walls' pain gate theory has made an immense contribution to our modern understanding of pain, describing it as a multi-dimensional experience, influenced by psychological and social factors. The contribution of Aaron Beck and the cognitive behavioural model has helped clinicians to explore new avenues of psychologically informed treatment approaches to back pain. Other key contributors to the approach we have discussed in this book include Professor Chris Main and Chris Spanswick, whose book *Pain Management* helped to guide the structure of the shorter programme we have developed in Birmingham, which is described in this book. Professor Paul Watson, Professor Kim Burton, Dr Nick Kendall, Dr Johannes Vlaeyen, Peter O'Sullivan and Dr Michael Sullivan have all added to our knowledge. They, and many others, who are included in the select reference list have helped to mould some of the key concepts of the biopsychosocial approach to clinical practice.

More recently, the influence of the late physiotherapist Louis Gifford in providing a practical way to apply the biopsychosocial approach for physiotherapists is highly significant. Physiotherapist and neuroscience expert Dr Lorimer Moseley has also made a significant contribution in helping us to understand and treat patients with persistent pain. His book, *Explain Pain*, co-written with David Butler, is a great resource for clinicians and anyone who wants to learn more about pain biology described in chapters 3 and 4 is encouraged to read this for further information, as this was and important source for developing our own understanding. Dr Mick Thacker, physiotherapist and neuroscience expert, has also been influential in helping us to understand the biology of persistent pain and his work continues to offer new and exciting insights into future treatments.

We are fortunate in the United Kingdom to have some high-quality research teams investigating biopsychosocial treatments for back pain and special mention must go to the research team at the Institute for Primary Care and Health Sciences at Keele University. Their research has helped us to predict which patients may be at risk of developing persistent back pain, and to design a new approach to managing these patients, taking into consideration psychological and social factors. Professor Sallie Lamb's research team at Warwick University has also researched this area of clinical practice and has demonstrated the effectiveness of this approach in patients with back pain.

We have both been fortunate to be able to apply the biopsychosocial approach within the occupational and insurance sector, spending several years working for Human Focus and Healthcare Risk Management. Our thanks go to the many people we worked with in these organisations.

The principles of The Human Givens Institute provide a framework for understanding what is essential for a person and a community to thrive and how to return people to good health using a biopsychosocial approach. Especial thanks go to The Human Givens College for their programme of education and training.

Thanks also to the Physiotherapy Pain Association, the British Pain Society and the Society for Back Pain Research for providing great conferences and education days to help further develop our knowledge.

And thanks also to our Editor at Random House, Morwenna Loughman, who has been with us every step of the way in preparing this book.

Finally, and most importantly, we would like to thank the many people we have seen with persistent back pain, who have chosen to engage with this treatment approach with an open mind and have worked hard to apply the principles described in this book. So many of them have seen their hard work rewarded with improvements in function and quality of life, and they continue to inspire us in using the biopsychosocial approach.

As clinicians, we firmly believe that it is only when we apply emerging research in daily clinical practice, and have the flexibility to learn, in a variety of healthcare settings, that we can truly test out different approaches to treating back pain. In the clinical setting, it can be challenging to filter all we know about the biopsychosocial model into care for our patients. For us, though, having navigated many different approaches to treating back pain, the biopsychosocial approach produces the best outcomes for patients with persistent back pain, and current high-quality research supports this.

If this book is able to give you a better insight into the biopsychosocial approach to back pain, it will have achieved its aims.

# FURTHER READING

If you are interested in reading more about this subject, the following key texts are useful.

Brown, G. and Winn, D., *Liberate Yourself from Pain – A Practical Help for Sufferers*, Human Givens Publishing, 2009. Many people we have worked with have acknowledged how helpful this text has been for their own recovery.

Burch V. *Living well with pain and illness. The mindful way to force yourself from suffering.* 2008. Piatkus.

Butler, D.S. and Moseley, G.L., *Explain Pain*, NOI Group Publications, 2013. An easy-to-read book that explores the biology of pain in detail, with useful illustrations.

Gifford, L.S., *Topical Issues in Pain. Volumes 1–5*, AuthorHouseUK, 2013. A useful text for clinicians which has transformed clinical practice using the biopsychosocial approach. It is written for clinicians so is quite technical.

Griffin J. and Tyrrell, I., *Human Givens – The New Approach to Emotional Health and Clear Thinking*, HG Publishing, 2013. This book brings together all that works in psychological therapies and links them to research from the neurosciences and outlines and excellent set of organising ideas

Main, C. and Spanswick, C., *Pain Management: An Interdisciplinary Approach*, Churchill Livingstone, 2000. An academic book for clinicians which encompasses a biopsychosocial approach to treating pain.

Moseley, G.L., *Painful Yarns: Metaphors and Stories to Help Understand the Biology of Pain*, NOI Group Publications, 2007. A collection of stories to help understanding of pain biology.

Waddell, G., *The Back Pain Revolution*, Churchill Livingstone 2004. A landmark academic text explaining the use of the biopsychosocial approach for back pain.

Wall, P., *Pain – The Science of Suffering*, Columbia University Press, 2000. A landmark book which brings everyday language to the science of pain.

## Useful websites and resources

http://www.pain-ed.com/ – a website for clinicians and the public with some useful resources including patient accounts of using the biopsychosocial approach

http://www.noigroup.com/en/Home – a website from the authors of *Explain Pain* with resources and blogs to help understand pain and how to address it using a biopsychosocial approach

http://knowpain.co.uk/wp-content/uploads/2014/05/ TazzyPersistentPainBooklet.pdf – a short booklet explaining pain biology and what to do to help yourself from a biopsychosocial perspective

*The therapeutic power of guided imagery.* CD available from www.humangivens.com

# REFERENCES

Altmaier, E.M., Lehmann, T.R., Russell, D.W., Weinstein, J.N., Feng Kao, C., 'The effectiveness of psychological interventions for the rehabilitation of low back pain: A randomized controlled trial evaluation', *Pain* 49: 329–335, 1992

Argueta-Bernal, G., 'Behavioral approaches for chronic low back pain', *Seminars in Pain Medicine* 2: 197–202, 2004

Ayre, M., Tyson, G., 'The role of self efficacy and fear avoidance beliefs in the prediction of disability', *Australian Psychology* 36: 250–253, 2001

Ballantyne, J.C., Kalso, E., Stannard, C., 'WHO analgesic ladder: a good concept gone astray. Our mistake is to treat chronic pain as if it were acute or end of life pain', *British Medical Journal*, 2016

Black, C., 'Working for a healthier tomorrow', The Stationery Office, London, 2008

Boden, S.D., et al., 'Abnormal magnetic-resonance scans of the lumbar spine in asymptomatic subjects: A prospective investigation', *The Journal of Bone and Joint Surgery*, Vol. 72, Issue 3, 403–408, 1990

Borenstein, D., et al., 'The Value of Magnetic Resonance Imaging of the Lumbar Spine to Predict Low-Back Pain in Asymptomatic Subjects: A Seven-Year Follow-up Study', *The Journal of Bone and Joint Surgery* (American) 83: 1306–1311, 2001

Brinjikji, W., Luetmer, P.H., Comstock, B., Bresnahan, B.W., Chen, L.E., Deyo, R.A., Halabi, S., Turner, J.A.,

Avins, A.L., James, K., Wald, J.T., Kallmes, D.F., Jarvik, J.G., 'Systematic Literature Review of Imaging Features of Spinal Degeneration in Asymptomatic Populations', *American Journal of Neuroradiology* 36: 811–816, 2015

Buchner, M., Zahlten-Hinguranage, A., Schiltenwolf, M., Neubauer, E., 'Therapy outcome after multidisciplinary treatment for chronic neck and chronic low back pain: a prospective clinical study in 365 patients', *Scandinavian Journal of Rheumatology*, Sep–Oct, 35(5): 363–367, 2006

Buer, N., Linton, S.J., 'Fear avoidance beliefs and catastrophising: occurrence and risk factor in back pain and ADL in the general population', *Pain* 99: 485–491, 2002

Burton, A.K., Tillotson, M.K., Main, C.J., Hollis, S., 'Psychosocial predictors of outcome in acute and subchronic low back trouble', *Spine* 20: 722–728, 1995

Clemes, S.A., 'What constitutes effective manual handling training? A systematic review', *Occupational Medicine* 60(2): 101–107, 2009

COST B13 Working Group on Guidelines for Chronic Low back Pain, 'European Guidelines for the management of chronic non-specific low back pain', European Commission Research Directorate General, 2004

Covington, E.C., 'The biological basis of pain', *International Review of Psychiatry* 12: 128–147, 2000

Crombez, G., Vlaeyen, J.W.S., Heuts, P.H.T.G., Lysens, R., 'Pain related fear is more disabling than pain itself: evidence on the role of pain related fear in chronic back disability', *Pain* 80: 329–339, 1999

CSAG, 'Clinical Standards Advisory Group report on back pain', HMSO Publications, London, 1994

Darlow, B., et al., 'Easy to Harm, Hard to Heal. Patient Views About the Back', *Spine* 40(11): 842–850, 2015

Deyo, R.A., von Korff, M., Duhrkoop, D., 'Opioids for low back pain', *British Medical Journal*, 2015

Engel, G., 'The need for a new medical model: a challenge for biomedicine', *Science* 196: 303–307, 1977

Fairbank, J.F., et al., 'Randomised controlled trial to compare surgical stabilisation of the lumbar spine with an intensive rehabilitation programme for patients with chronic low back pain: the MRC spine stabilisation trial', *British Medical Journal*, 2005

Flor, H., Fydrich, T., Turk, D.C., 'Efficacy of multidisciplinary pain treatment centers: a meta-analytic review', *Pain* 49: 221–230, 1992

Fordyce, W.E., 'Learning processes in pain' in R.A. Sternback (ed.), *The Psychology of Pain*, 49–72. Raven Press, New York, 1976

Frank, J.W., Kerr, M.S., Brooker, A.S., 'Disability resulting from occupational low back pain', *Spine* 21: 2908–2929, 1996

Fritz, J.M., George, S.Z., 'Identifying psychosocial variables in patients with acute work related low back pain: the importance of fear avoidance beliefs', *Physical Therapy* 82: 973–983, 2002

Gatchel, R.J., Polatin, P.B., Noe, C., Gardea, M., Pulliam, C., Thompson, J., 'Treatment and cost-effectiveness of early intervention for acute low back pain patients: a one year prospective study', *Journal of Occupational Rehabilitation* 13: 1–10, 2003

Gifford, L., 'Pain, the Tissues and the Nervous System: A conceptual model', *Physiotherapy* 84(1): 27–36, 1998

Guzman, J., Esmail, R., Karjalainen, K., Malmivaara, A., Irvin, E., Bombardier, C., 'Multidisciplinary rehabilitation for low back pain: a systematic review', *British Medical Journal* 322: 1511–1516, 2001

Hansen, Z., Daykin, A., Lamb, S.E., 'A cognitive-behavioural programme for the management of low back pain in primary care: a description and justification of the intervention used in the Back Skills Training Trial', *Physiotherapy* 96: 87–94, 2010

Harding, V., Williams, Amanda C. de C., 'Extending Physiotherapy Skills Using a Psychological Approach: Cognitive-behavioural management of chronic pain', *Physiotherapy* 81(11): 681–688, 1995

Hashmi, Javeria A., Baliki, Marwan N., Huang, Lejian, Baria, Alex T., Torbey, Souraya, Hermann, Kristina M., Schnitzer, Thomas J., Apkarian, A. Vania, 'Shape shifting pain: chronification of back pain shifts brain representation from nociceptive to emotional circuits', *Brain* 136: 2751–2768, 2013

Hay, E.M., Mullis, R., Lewis, M., Vohara, K., Watson, P., Dzeidzic, K.M., Sim, J., Minns-Low, C., Croft, P.R., 'Comparison of physical treatments versus a brief pain management intervention for back pain in primary care: a randomized clinical trial in physiotherapy practice, *The Lancet* 365: 2024–2030, 2005

Hill et al., 'A Primary Care Back Pain Screening Tool: Identifying Patient Subgroups for Initial Treatment', *Arthritis & Rheumatism* 59(5): 632–641, 2008

Hill et al., 'Comparison of stratified primary care management for low back pain with current best practice (STarT Back): a randomised controlled trial', *The Lancet*, 2011

Hunter et al., 'Evaluation of a functional restoration programme in chronic low back pain', *Occupational Medicine*
56: 497–500, 2006

Hurley, D.A., Tully, M.A., Lonsdale, C., Boreham,
C.A., van Mechelen, W., Daly, L., Tynan, A.,
McDonough, S.M., 'Supervised walking in comparison
with fitness training for chronic back pain in physiotherapy: results of the SWIFT single-blinded randomized
controlled trial', *Pain* 156(1): 131–147, 2015

Jellama, P., van der Windt, D., van der Horst, H., Twisk, J.,
Stalman, W., Bouter, L., 'Should treatment of (sub) acute
low back pain be aimed at psychosocial prognostic factors?
Cluster randomised clinical trial in general practice', *British
Medical Journal* 331: 84–88, 2005

Jensen, M.P., Turner, J.A., Romano, J.M., Karoly, P.,
'Coping with chronic pain. A critical review of the literature', *Pain* 47: 249–283, 1991

Jensen, M., et al., 'Magnetic Resonance Imaging of the
Lumbar Spine in People without Back Pain', *New England
Journal of Medicine* 331: 69–73, 1994

Johannsen, E., Lindberg, P., 'Clinical application of
physiotherapy with a cognitive-behavioural approach
in low back pain', *Advances in Physiotherapy*
3: 3–17, 2001

Johnson, R.E., Jones, G.T., Wiles, N.J., Chaddock, C.,
Potter, R.G., Roberts, C., Symmons, D.P.M., Watson, P.J.,
Torgerson, D.J., Macfarlan, G.J., 'Active exercise, edu-
cation, and cognitive behavioral therapy for persistent
disabling low back pain: A randomized controlled trial',
*Spine* 32: 1578–1585, 2007

Kaapa, E.H., Frantsi, K., Sarna, S., Malmivaara, A.,
'Multidisciplinary group rehabilitation versus individual

physiotherapy for chronic nonspecific low back pain: a randomized trial', *Spine* 31: 371–377, 2006

Kamper et al., 'Multidisciplinary biopsychosocial rehabilitation for chronic low back pain: Cochrane systematic review and meta-analysis', *British Medical Journal*, 2015

Keefe, F.J., 'Cognitive behavioural therapy for managing pain', *The Clinical Psychologist* 49: 4–5, 1996

Kendall, N., Linton, S., Main, C.J., 'Guide to assessing psychological yellow flags in acute low back pain: risk factors for long term disability and work loss', Accident Rehabilitation and Compensation Insurance Corporation of New Zealand and the National Health Committee, Wellington, New Zealand, 1997

Klaber-Moffett et al., 'Randomised controlled trial of exercise for low back pain: clinical outcomes, costs, and preferences', *British Medical Journal*, 2006

Lamb et al., 'Group cognitive behavioural treatment for low-back pain in primary care: a randomised controlled trial and cost-effectiveness analysis', *The Lancet* 375, 2010

Lee, M.I., Silverman, S.M., Hansen, H., Patel, V.B., Manchikanti, L., 'A comprehensive review of opioid-induced hyperalgesia', *Pain Physician* 14(2): 145–161, 2011

Lethem, J., Slade, P.D., Troup, J.D.G., Bentley, G., 'Outline of a fear avoidance model of exaggerated pain perception', *Behavioural Research Therapy* 21: 401–408, 1983

Lindstrom, I., Ohlund, C., Eek, C., 'The effect of graded activity on patients with sub-acute low back pain. A randomized prospective clinical study with an operant conditioning-behavioural approach', *Physical Therapy* 72: 279–293, 1992

Linton, S.J., *Understanding pain for better clinical practice*, Elsevier, Edinburgh, 2005

Linton, S.J., Andersson, T., 'Can chronic disability be prevented? A randomized controlled trial of a cognitive behavioural intervention and two forms of information for patients with spinal pain', *Spine* 25: 2825–2831, 2000

Linton, S.J., Bradley, L.A., 'Strategies for the prevention of chronic pain' in Gatchel, R.J. and Turk, D.C. (eds), *Psychological approaches to pain management: a practitioners handbook*, Guildford Press, New York, 1996

Linton, S.J., Boersma, K., Jansson, M., Lennart, S., Botvalde, M., 'The effects of cognitive behavioural and physical therapy preventative interventions on pain related sick leave: A randomized controlled trial', *Clinical Journal of Pain* 21: 109–119, 2005

Main, C.J., Watson, P.J., 'Psychological aspects of pain', *Manual Therapy* 4(4): 203–215, 1999

Main et al., 'Integrating physical and psychological approaches to treatment in low back pain: the development and content of the STarT Back trial's "high-risk" intervention', *Physiotherapy*, 2011

Marhold, C., Linton, S.J., Melin, L., 'A cognitive behavioural return to work programme: effects on pain patients with a history of long-term versus short-term sick leave', *Pain* 91: 155–163, 2001

Mayer TG, Gatchel RJ (1998) Functional Restoration for spinal disorders: the sports medicine approach Lea and Febiger, Philadelphia.

McCracken, L.M., 'Learning to live with the pain: acceptance of pain predicts adjustment in persons with chronic pain', *Pain* 74: 21–27, 1998

Melzack, R., *Pain assessment and measurement*, Raven Press, New York, 1983

Melzack, R., 'From the gate to the neuromatrix', *Pain* S121–S126, 1999

Melzack, R. and Wall, P.D., *The challenge of pain* (2nd edition), Penguin, London, 1996

Menzel, N.N., Robinson, M.E., 'Back pain in direct patient care providers: Early intervention with cognitive behavioral therapy', *Pain Management Nursing* 7: 53–63, 2006

Moore, J., Von Korff, M., Cherkin, D., Saunders, K., Lorig, K., 'A randomized trial of a cognitive behavioural program for enhancing back pain self care in a primary care setting', *Pain* 88: 145–153, 2000

Morley, S., Ecclestone, C., Williams, A., 'A systematic review and meta-analysis of randomized controlled trials of cognitive behaviour therapy and behaviour therapy for chronic pain in adults, excluding headache', *Pain* 80: 1–13, 1999

Moseley, G.L., 'Combined physiotherapy and education is efficacious for chronic low back pain', *Australian Journal of Physiotherapy* 48, 2002

Moseley, G.L., 'A pain neuromatrix approach to patients with chronic pain', *Manual Therapy* 8(3): 130–140, 2003

Moseley, G.L., et al., 'A Randomized Controlled Trial of Intensive Neurophysiology Education in Chronic Low Back Pain', *Clinical Journal of Pain* 20(5): 324–330, 2004

National Institute of Health and Care Excellence, 'Low back pain in adults: early management', CG88, 2009

National Institute of Health and Care Excellence, 'Physical activity: brief advice for adults in primary care', PH44, 2013

National Institute of Health and Care Excellence, 'Headaches in over-12's: diagnosis and management', CG150, 2012

O'Sullivan, P., 'It's time for change with the management of non-specific chronic low back pain', *British Journal of Sports Medicine*, 2011

Pengel, H.M., Maher, C.G., Refshauge, K.M., 'Systematic review of conservative interventions for subacute low back pain', *Pain Reviews* 9: 153–164, 2002

Peterson-Felix, S., et al., 'Neuroplasticity – an important factor in acute and chronic pain', *Swiss Med Weekly* 132: 273–278, 2002

Pincus, T., Burton, A.K., Vogel, S., 'A systematic review of psychological factors as predictors of chronicitity disability in prospective cohorts of low back pain', *Spine* 27: E109–120, 2002

Pincus, T., Vlaeyen, J.A., Kendall, N., 'Cognitive behavioural therapy and psychosocial factors in low back pain: directions for the future', *Spine* 27: E133–138, 2002

Ranson, C.A., 'Magnetic resonance imaging of the lumbar spine in asymptomatic professional fast bowlers in cricket', *Journal of Bone and Joint Surgery* (British), Vol. 87-B, Issue 8, 1111–1116, 2015

Rogers et al., 'A Retrospective Analysis of a Functional Restoration Service for Patients with Persistent Low Back Pain', *Musculoskeletal Care*, 2014

Royal College of General Practitioners, *Clinical guidelines for the management of acute low back pain*, RCGP, London, 1999

Schonstein, E., Kenny, D.T., Keating, J.L., Koes, B.W., 'Work conditioning, work hardening and functional restoration for workers with back and neck pain', *Cochrane Database of Systematic Reviews* 3: CD001822-NaN, 2003

Sowden et al., 'Subgrouping for targeted treatment in primary care for low back pain: the treatment system and clinical training programmes used in the IMPaCT Back study', *Family Practice* 1–13, 2011

Sullivan, M.J., Stanish, W., 'Psychologically based occupational rehabilitation: The pain disability prevention programme', *Clinical Journal of Pain* 19(2): 97–104, 2003

Trelle, S., Reichenbach, S., Wandel, S., Hildebrand, P., Tschannen, B., Villiger, P.M., Egger, M., Jüni, P., 'Cardiovascular safety of non-steroidal anti-inflammatory drugs: network meta-analysis', *SOBMJ* 342: c7086, 2011

Turk, D.C., Meichenbaum, D.H., Genest, M., *Pain and behavioural medicine: a cognitive behavioural perspective*, The Guildford Press, New York, 1983

Turk, D.C., Okifuji, A.D., 'A cognitive behavioural approach to pain management', in Wall, P.D., Melzack, R. (eds), *Textbook of Pain*, Churchill Livingstone, London, 1999, 1431–1444

Turner, J.A., Clancy, S., 'Strategies for coping with chronic low back pain: Relationship to pain and disability', *Pain* 24: 355–364, 1986

Van den Hout, J.H., Vlaeyen, J.W.S., Heuts, P.H.T.G., Sillen, W.J.T., Wilkie, A.J.E., 'Functional disability in low back pain. The role of pain related fear and problem solving skills', *International Journal of Behavioural Medicine* 8: 134–148, 2001

Van der Windt, D., Hay, E., Jellema, P., Main, C., 'Psychosocial interventions for low back pain in primary care', *Spine* 33: 1–8, 2007

Vibe Fersum, K., O'Sullivan, P., Skouen, J.S., Smith, A., Kvåle, A., 'Efficacy of classification-based cognitive functional therapy in patients with non-specific chronic low back pain: A randomized controlled trial', *European Journal of Pain* 17: 916–928, 2013

Viennau, T.L., Clark, A.J., Lynch, M.E., Sullivan, M.J.L., 'Catastrophizing, functional disability, and pain reports in adults with chronic low back pain', *Pain Research and Management* 4: 93–96, 1999

Vlaeyen, J.W.S., Kole-Snijders, A.M.J., Rotteveel, A.M., Ruesink, R., Heuts, P.H.T.G., 'The role of fear of movement/(re)injury in pain disability', *Journal of Occupational Rehabilitation* 5: 235–252, 1995

Waddell, G., *Models of disability: using low back pain as an example*, Royal Society of Medicine Press, London, 2002

Waddell, G., *The back pain revolution*, Churchill Livingstone, Edinburgh, 2004

Waddell, G., Newton, M., Henderson, I., Somerville, D., Main, C., 'A fear avoidance beliefs questionnaire and the role of fear avoidance in chronic low back pain and disability', *Pain* 52: 157–168, 1993

Waddell, G., Burton, A.K., 'Occupational health guidelines for the management of low back pain at work', Faculty of Occupational Medicine, London, 2000

Waddell, G., Burton, A.K., 'Concepts of rehabilitation for the management of common health problems', The Stationery Office, London, 2004

Zusman, M., 'Cognitive-behavioural components of musculoskeletal physiotherapy', *Physical Therapy Reviews* 10: 89–98, 2005

# INDEX